The First 30 Years

A JOURNEY OF FAITH

KENNETH COPELAND PUBLICATIONS

FORT WORTH, TEXAS

The First 30 Years
A Journey of Faith

ISBN 1-57562-189-4   30-0706

All scripture is from the *King James Version* unless otherwise noted.

Kenneth Copeland Publications
Fort Worth, Texas 76192-0001

Dedication

This book is dedicated to the faithfulness

of the Partners and friends of Kenneth Copeland Ministries.

Your hearing from God, and being obedient to His instruction

to uphold KCM in prayer and with your gifts, has empowered people all

over the world to go from the milk of the Word to the meat of the Word,

and from religion to reality. Lives have been changed forever!

Thank you for your love and support, and for being the

most faithful Partners in the world!

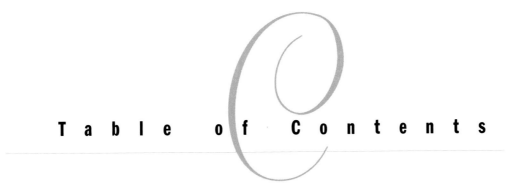

Table of Contents

Introduction

It's been more than 30 years now since Brother Copeland stood in the dried-up Arkansas River bed and received God's call to ministry. It's been 30 years since God commissioned him to preach the uncompromised Word from the top of the world to the bottom and all the way around. It's been 30 years since Kenneth and Gloria Copeland began their journey of faith.

That's exactly what it's been—a journey that has required faith every step of the way. It's been a journey as real as the one the Israelites took from Egypt to their Promised Land.

According to the Bible, the children of Israel stopped periodically during their journey to set up stone memorials as a reminder of God's faithfulness. One of the times they built such a memorial was after they crossed the Jordan River. The book of Joshua tells how the priests stood holding the Ark of the Covenant in the riverbed to keep back the water while Joshua started work on the memorial. He sent one man from each tribe into the riverbed to pick up stones, carry them out of the river and build a memorial to God.

And he spake unto the children of Israel, saying, When your children shall ask their fathers in time to come, saying, What mean these stones?

Then ye shall let your children know, saying, Israel came over this Jordan on dry land.

For the Lord your God dried up the waters of the Jordan from before you, until ye were passed over, as the Lord your God did to the Red sea, which he dried up from before us, until we were gone over.

That all the people of the earth might know the hand of the Lord, that it is mighty: that ye might fear the Lord your God for ever (Joshua 4:21-24).

The purpose of a memorial was two-fold. First, it was a reminder to the children of Israel and to all the surrounding people of the power and might of the one, true God. Second, it was a witness of His faithfulness to future generations.

Today, we as believers are blessed to be living under an even better covenant with God. The Bible calls us "living stones." Therefore, our lives should be a living testimony, both to our generation and to the next, of God's goodness.

Those of us on the staff at Kenneth Copeland Ministries believe the lives of Kenneth and Gloria Copeland are indeed such a testimony. And since this year marks their 30th year of ministry, we think it's a good time to commemorate God's faithfulness to them. What better time to look back and remember what has happened during this journey of faith and what God has done for them thus far?

As all of us who know the Copelands have discovered, it is virtually impossible to convince either of them to sit down and talk (much less write) about themselves. So we've taken the liberty of putting together this scrapbook of memories for them. We've taken our favorite stories—ones they've told from the pulpit many times—added a few others from friends and family, then put them alongside some special photos, both old and new.

We're grateful the Copelands allowed us to do so. For even though they'd never compare themselves to Joshua, those of us who have been blessed by their lives do see a similarity. We see in them people who dared to believe God. People who dared to follow Him by faith. And their obedience has helped many of us find our way into God's land of promise.

Of course, we hope this book will bring a smile to all those who love the Copelands as we do. But above all, we pray it will bring glory to the God and Father of our Lord Jesus Christ Who has blessed us all with every blessing both in heaven and on earth. To Him be all the praise for the great things He has done to help each one of us along our journey of faith.

The Staff of Kenneth Copeland Ministries

CHAPTER 1

The Early Years

But when He who had set me apart, even from my mother's womb, and called me

through His grace, was pleased to reveal His Son in me, that I might preach Him…

GALATIANS 1:15

God has a divine plan and purpose for every person ever conceived on this earth. Some discover that plan. Others don't.

Left to myself, I never would have gone God's way. I never would have lived out His plan. But I wasn't left to myself. I had a mother who loved God and was doggedly determined from the day I was born that I would serve Him.

All the time I was growing up, she and my daddy saw to it that I went to church. I wasn't grateful. In fact, I fought it the whole time. I didn't like being cooped up in that musty, old church house. Outside, the day would be bright and sunshiny. Other kids would be playing ball and having fun, but I was stuck inside learning memory verses that I didn't understand.

Of course, years later I figured out that the words of those verses were powerful and true. I found out that when you mix faith with them, they can change your life, your circumstances or anything else that needs changing. I didn't know that back then, and if someone had tried to tell me, I probably wouldn't have listened.

On Sunday night, we'd go back to church for Training Union and they'd

(Facing page) A.W. and Vinita Copeland with Kenneth in June, 1939, Abilene, Texas. Kenneth was 3½ years old.

As a kid, my primary talent was the talent of mess-up. I could mess up more than you could fix. My mama learned quickly never to leave a clock or radio in my bedroom. After everyone was in bed and asleep, I'd still be awake listening to that clock tick. To me it sounded like this, *Tick…Tock…Take…Me…Apart…*

I couldn't stand it. The clock wouldn't last three days. I had to find out what in the world was inside it, and what made it work. I'd pull the thing in bed with me and start tearing it apart.

The problem was, I could never get it back together. I had trouble in that area. I'd get things apart, but I could never figure out how to fix them. That was my talent—fouling up. I succeeded in fouling up for many years, until I finally got desperate and made Jesus the Lord of my life.

Once I did that, the God-given character trait that had previously worked against me started working for me! It caused me to go after the Word of God just like I did those clocks. I just *had* to find out how it worked. The best part was, I had the Holy Spirit helping me. He taught me how to use faith in the Word the way a mechanic uses a wrench or a carpenter uses a hammer. He taught me how to stop tearing things up and start fixing them for a change.

Kenneth

ask us what we learned that morning. I never learned anything, because I was mad all the time. Early on, I made up my mind that if I ever got bigger than my mama, I would never go back.

Obviously, God (and Mama) had other plans.

I'll admit, I was an angry, stubborn young man before I was born again. In fact, at times I was an outright terror. But I came by it honestly. I came from a whole line of men just like me.

My great-grandfather, for example, was a full-blooded Cherokee Indian known as Cussin' Owens. He left the Indian way of life when he was young and became an Army scout and buffalo hunter. He was meaner than a junkyard dog.

I read an account of his life written in the back of one of the family Bibles. It said that during the Civil War, when he was only 13 or 14 years old, a Yankee officer strung him up by his thumbs to make him tell where his daddy and uncle were. They spit in his face and cussed him. He screamed and cussed them back. No matter what they did to him, he cussed and screamed louder. He wouldn't stop. They said he *invented* cuss words.

You might say he earned his name.

Later in his life, he married and had children, one of whom was my grandfather. But that didn't mellow him much. He was such a hard disciplinarian, he sometimes used a black snake whip to punish his kids.

When my grandfather was about 9 years old, he stood up to Cussin' Owens. He later told his mother, "Mama, I'm leaving home today, because if he ever hits me with that black snake whip again, I'll kill him—and I don't want his blood on my hands." At that very young age, he left home and never went back.

But even in those days, God was working in my family. He started by getting hold of my great-grandmother. (I believe God often starts with women because they're so tenacious. He knows once they get after their family for God,

they won't stop until the job is done. Women just don't know how to quit!)

My great-grandmother never called her husband by his first name. She called him "Mr. Owens." I remember she used to wear a black bonnet and a full-length black dress that flared all the way to the ground.

One time, my aunt, who was her youngest daughter, said, "Kenneth, I remember when Mama went *holiness.*" I jerked my head around. That was news to me.

"*What did you say,* Aunt Pinky?"

"I said I can remember when Mama went holiness." That's what they called people back then who'd been baptized in the Holy Ghost.

"Sure enough?"

"Yeah," Aunt Pinky said, "she used to get up in the morning, fix breakfast and get the men out to the fields. Then, she'd get the older kids off to school and send the others outside. Back then, the houses had heavy wooden shutters that you could close up for protection. Well, she'd close all the shutters and shut herself into the back room of the house. Kenneth, you never heard such moaning and groaning in all your life! What do you reckon she was doing? Do you think she was praying?"

"Sure she was, Aunt Pinky."

"Do you really think so?"

"I know so," I said. When I looked back on it, I realized that this happened in the early 1900s. The Spirit of God was being poured out all over this country. The revival at Azusa Street had just exploded. There was revival all over this nation. The Spirit of God was moving out there in that Texas cow country, but most people didn't realize it. My great-grandmother did, though. By the time my mama was born in 1911, the revival was in full bloom.

I remember Mama saying that she would climb up on the windmill and pray, and pray, and pray. Then she and her cousins would go down to the cellar where they could sing and shout and no one would hear them.

When all was said and done, my great-grandmother had accumulated quite a track record. She got every one of her children saved. Every member of the family, some through the influence of my mama's prayers, was born again. They *all* came to God through that old woman's prayers.

She even got my Great-Grandfather Owens. I understand he got saved shortly before he died.

That goes to show you, if God can just find someone with some faith who is willing to pray, He can do anything.

Kenneth

When I was little, clothes were a problem for me. They were made strangely back then—the shirt buttoned to the britches! Can you imagine how uncomfortable it would be to have your shirt buttoned to your pants? I remember the first time I ever dressed myself. I was just a little guy, about 3 or 4 years old, and Mama had just gone down to the corner grocery store. I decided to dress myself and surprise Mama when she got home.

I *still* remember what a chore it was trying to get those clothes on and buttoned right. I mean, I *worked* at it, and it took a long time. When I finished, they were twisted every which way, and everything was buttoned wrong.

Oddly enough, I thought about that when I first started trying to walk by faith in the Word. The smallest thing seemed to be tough. But, like Mama, God was gracious and even though I made mistakes, He appreciated the effort.

Eventually I found that the Word of God fit me far better than those silly button-down outfits ever did. So as I got into the habit of believing it and acting on it, things just started falling in place for me.

I'm so glad that God created us with the ability to form habits. I've learned that it's the *habitual* things in our lives that create excellence. And the best habit you can have is the habit of living by faith in the Word of God. It should be as much a part of your life as getting dressed.

Kenneth

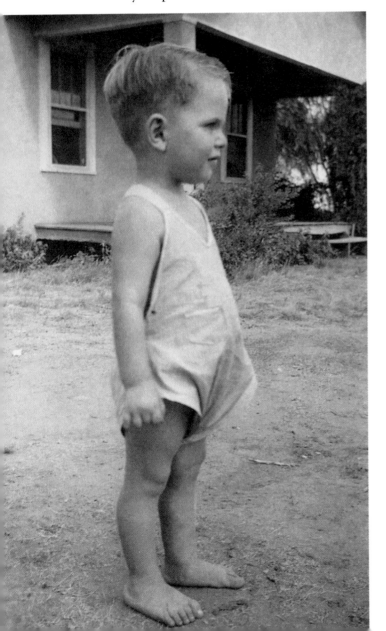

Kenneth circa 1938
Abilene, Texas.

hen I was a young boy, my dad was gone a lot. He traveled for a living and I missed him. The day he was scheduled to come home, I couldn't do anything except look for him. I watched for him all the time.

The only thing more exciting than having Daddy home was hearing him say, "Kenneth, in the morning, we're going to get up early and go fishing."

Life didn't get any better than going fishing with Daddy.

I'd rush in to tell Mama. "Daddy and I are going fishing in the morning!"

I'd get so excited I couldn't sleep. I'd get up in the middle of the night to make sure my tackle box was still sitting there. I'd lay out the clothes I was going to wear. By 3 or 4 in the morning, I was up and

dressed with fishing gear in each hand.

I was *ready* to go fishing!

Of course, some days Daddy had other things he wanted me to do. He would come home and say, "Kenneth, we're going to get up early tomorrow and work in the yard."

Aw, Dad!

Working in the yard has always been my idea of absolutely nothing to do. On those days, I didn't look for my yard-working clothes. I didn't wake up once during the night. When Daddy came to wake me up, I'd be sound asleep. I was never up smiling and ready to go. Not once did I ever have a hoe in my hand before Daddy got up. He usually had to wake me up several times.

I fell asleep on the floor while I was tying my shoes.

I fell asleep at the breakfast table.

I felt sick at my stomach and complained loud and long about it.

I'd be asleep on my feet at 6 in the morning. I usually didn't wake up completely until almost noon, and by then I was hurting all over.

Think about that for a minute.

What made the difference?

It was the same man. I loved my dad as much as I'd loved him the day we went fishing. The weather could be identical. The same kind of day.

The only difference?

My will.

I didn't *will* to work in the yard.

The Lord has reminded me of the difference between fishing days and yard days many times since I've been born again and in the ministry.

Some things just don't change.

I still thoroughly dislike working in the yard.

Only now, the stakes are much bigger.

My *will* determines whether I act in faith or in fear.

My *will* determines whether I act on what God said or what the devil said.

And so does yours. What will *you* decide?

Kenneth

During World War II, school students bought savings stamps with their lunch money. There were red ones and blue ones, about the size of a postage stamp. The blue ones were worth more than the red ones.

We bought our stamps and put them in a book. Everyone had a book. You had to have a ration book to eat, a gas ration book to drive—you couldn't do anything without a book. The red and blue stamps were savings stamps. Later, S&H Green Stamps got their idea from the government.

You were supposed to put your stamps in your book, then when it was full, you could get a savings bond. Since there was a war on, they were called "war bonds." After the war, they turned into "savings bonds." You could buy a war bond for $18.75, and in 10 years it would be worth $25.

Everybody was putting stamps in their book. Those savings stamp books were supposed to be all of one color—either red or blue. When I filled up my book and turned it in, the teachers always went bananas. I'd have one page of red stamps. One page of blue stamps. I'd have another page that was half red and half blue. My book was so fouled up, they couldn't figure out if they owed me or if I owed them.

That's a good example of how I handled my finances when I was 8 years old. When Gloria came across me, I hadn't changed much. I still had things confused. My books were so fouled up, I like to have never gotten a war bond.

As an adult, I handled my finances the same way. I did what a lot of people are still doing. I lived on 120 percent of my income by borrowing money and paying little or none of the bill when it came due. That's common practice—it's also dishonest.

My dad was great at handling money. He absolutely walked in wisdom about finances. He did things in business that astonished people. He came up with answers nobody had considered.

You know why I handled money so badly? Nobody ever taught me any other way. My dad traveled all the time, and Mama wasn't any better than I was. Both of us could get into a financial mess, and Daddy would have to come home and straighten it out.

What should have been happening in my life? Somebody over at the church should have been teaching financial integrity from the Word of God. Because that's where we were. Dad was out of town, but Mama and I were at that church all the time.

If anyone tried to talk about finances they'd run him off. "We don't want preachers to talk about money!"

Yet, the whole bunch was financially destitute. Being financially destitute doesn't necessarily have anything to do with income. You would think that a fellow worth a billion dollars could make his house payments, but I know of one who had his home foreclosed recently. If you don't learn to live on what you have, there will never be enough.

The Lord said that if we are faithful over small things, He will make us rulers over much. That's the way the Church is going to have to get out of debt—one step of integrity at a time.

Kenneth

At 17, Kenneth was singing in high school concerts. The *Fort Worth Star-Telegram* reported he sang his first solo at age 10.

Looking back, I realize that there were times in my teenage years when the anointing of God came on me—even though I wasn't saved. I didn't know what it was, and I certainly didn't have any control over it. It usually happened when my mother put pressure on me to sing in church. I *disliked* doing that.

I'd stand outside the building and smoke until the service started. Then when I went in to sing—probably because of my mother's prayers—the anointing would come on my voice. It wasn't coming from the *inside* of me, because it wasn't in there. It came *upon* me.

It may seem hard to imagine that God would use me when I wasn't saved, but remember, the Bible says He used a jackass one time (Numbers 22:27-33). He straightened out a prophet with the mouth of a mule. Back then, there wasn't much difference between me and a mule.

I remember thinking, *If I could sing like this on Saturday night, I'd make a fortune.*

Some of the guys asked me, "Copeland, why don't you sing that way in the clubs?"

"Do you think I'm crazy?" I asked. "I've *tried!*"

Still, I didn't like singing in church. One time when I was somewhere between 20 and 22 years old, Mama asked me to sing and I said, "No, I'm not going! I don't like to mess with those people. They're goofy."

"Well, that's all right," she said, and left the room.

A while later my dad came in. "I want to ask you something, boy," he said. "When you were living at home, did you ever get up in the morning when there weren't clean clothes in your closet?"

"No, sir."

"Did you ever go in that kitchen when she didn't have your breakfast ready?"

"No, sir."

"Did you ever…"

He didn't have to say anything else. I'd gotten the message. "OK, Dad…I'll sing at the meeting."

Kenneth

Vinita Pearl Owens Copeland (1911-1988). Pictured here at age 14.

I don't like to think about where I would have ended up if my mother hadn't laid down her life for me in prayer. I was headed for hell as fast as I could go. But Mother would get in prayer sometimes and stay there for days and *days.*

"Daddy," I asked one time, "doesn't Mama ever *sleep?*"

"Son," he said, "she never even wrinkles the sheets."

She had physical problems on and off most all her life. Her appendix ruptured when she was a teenage girl. They all thought surely she would die, but she refused. However, it left her all messed up on the inside. The doctors told her when she was about 30 years old that she wouldn't live. They told her the same thing when she was 40.

"You'll never live another 10 years," they said when she was 50.

She lived all right, but she spent her life praying like she was going to die. She'd pray all night long. She prayed all the time. She'd *pray…pray…pray.* She later said when she was in her 70s, "If I'd known I was going to live so long, I would have taken better care of myself."

She spent years praying for me. Finally, she got fed up. She walked into the kitchen, slammed her Bible on the table and hollered at God, "I'm through praying for him! If he goes to hell it's Your fault, not mine! I've prayed every prayer I know how to pray!"

She didn't know it then, but she'd just released her faith.

I was saved three weeks later.

Afterward she said, "You know, I've had the driest three weeks spiritually that I've ever had."

"How come, Mama?" I asked.

"Since you got saved, I don't have hardly anything to pray about."

But before long she was hard at it again. She prayed in every member of the family. Then, she prayed in all my friends. If she ever got on your case, it was better to save yourself some hard knocks and go ahead and give your life to God.

After I'd gone into the ministry, the Lord spoke to me. *If I have to get you up every morning and put you to bed every night,* He said, *you are not going to fail.*

"I sure appreciate that, Lord," I said, "but *why me?* Better men than me have failed."

Because I have your mama in My face.

He was serious about it, too. He said, *She is constantly talking to Me about you. So you're going to make it if I have to get you up every morning and put you to bed every night.*

He did it, too. He got on *my* case, because Mama was on *His* case.

Thank God for praying mamas.

Kenneth

I realized that I was called into the ministry when I was a teenager. The only problem was that I'd never been born again. That seems peculiar because I was raised in the church. We weren't just there every time the doors were open, my mama had *a key!* We were there when the door was opened, and we were there any time she *wanted* the door opened.

Yet it never dawned on me to make Jesus the Lord of my life. Since we were a repenting church, every time I got to feeling bad, I'd just tell God I was sorry. Then I'd sign a rededication card. They had quite a stack of cards on me!

Still, even unsaved kids pick up on the things of God in the atmosphere of a Christian home. So, although I had never been born again, I knew by the time I was a teenager that I was called to the ministry. I also knew that I needed someone to help me. I drove down to the church and said, "I believe that God's called me to the ministry. Between now and when I graduate from high school, I'd like to work here at the church and learn some things so that maybe I'll know where to go to school."

"No," I was told, "you can't do that."

"Why?" I asked.

"It's taken us over 20 years to develop the reputation of this church, and we don't want a tramp like you tearing it down."

I was just a kid, and that hurt *bad.* By the time I got to my car, I was mad. By the time I got my car started, I was looking for someone to hit. I drove around all afternoon cussing, spitting, griping and cussing some more.

"They don't want me!" I shouted. "Well, I don't want them! They're all a bunch of blockheaded hypocrites."

I felt like I had a legal right to talk that way. When I look back on it now, I don't blame the church leaders for feeling the way they did. But they didn't handle it right.

I drove around until later that night, and then I went to a nightclub in town. Boy, the devil set me up.

I walked through the door of that place, and it was wall-to-wall people. When I stepped inside, the owner hollered loud enough that the band stopped playing. "There's the man who will never have to pay for drinks in my joint as long as he lives if he'll just sing when I ask him to!"

Wasn't that a setup?

All I could think was, *They want me, but the Christians don't.*

I spent the next nine years singing in those joints.

Kenneth

Kenneth singing in the Spring Follies, 1954.

By the time I was a teenager, I'd rebelled against both my parents and God. I spent my time singing in night-clubs and joints hoping to make it big in music.

Then, in 1957 when I was 20 years old, I recorded a song called "Pledge of Love."

I *knew* that song was going to make it, and make it big.

What I didn't realize back then was that I couldn't be a real success at anything in life as long as I was running from God. And I was hoofing it as far from Him as I could get! I was so far from being where God wanted me to be and preaching what He wanted me to preach, that I might as well have been in the belly of a whale just like Jonah.

As a private in the U.S. Army stationed at Fort Gordon, Georgia, Kenneth sang "Pledge of Love" on Steve Allen's network television show. It was 1957 and the local paper said he'd "hit the big time."

Would you like to know what happened *the day the record was released?*

I got drafted.

I was in the Army watching that record climb on the charts each day, until it reached the *Top Ten,* and sold 300,000 copies. At the pinnacle of its success, when I should have been releasing my next recording, I was doing push-ups for Uncle Sam.

By the time I was discharged from the Army, the song had dropped off the charts and my name had been forgotten.

I didn't realize it then, but *nothing* I set my hand to do would succeed until I got my heart right. Years later, I experienced something greater than a hundred gold albums. I discovered the *true* "Pledge of Love."

The author was Jesus.

It was released on a Cross.

It was recorded in heaven.

Finally, once and for all time, I put my life in His hands.

He gave me His Name—forever.

He promised *never* to leave me.

He promised me life, and life *abundantly.*

I discovered that I was in covenant with the King of kings…the Lord of lords…the Prince of Peace. The God of the universe.

Now, *that's* success.

Kenneth

A page from *"Dig"* magazine, 1957, described the rising young singer as an entertainment star of tomorrow.

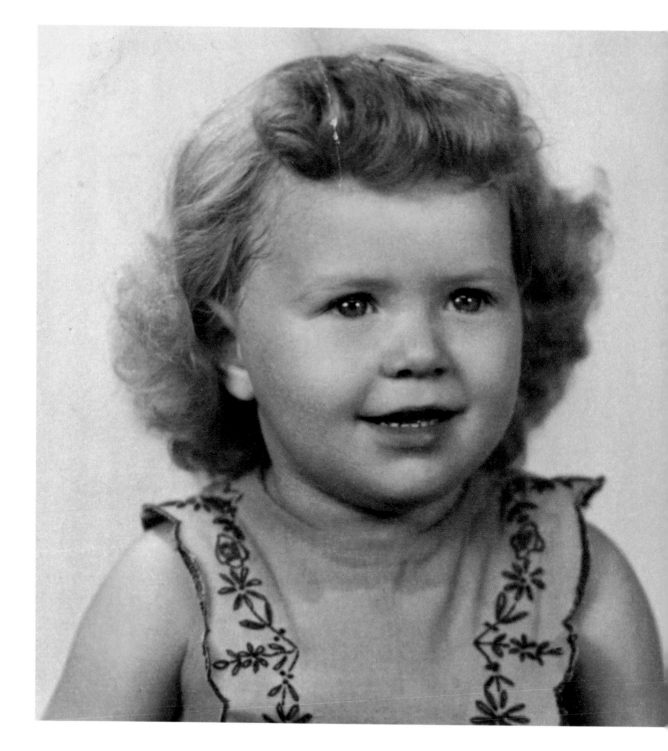

Gloria, age 3, in a dress her mother made.

I grew up in Center Point, Arkansas, so long ago they didn't even have a hospital in the area. They used to have a population of 144. But over time, things change. It got smaller.

I was raised in a church where they said miracles had passed away. As a little girl, I didn't know any better than that. I wasn't very good about going to church when I was young. I'm really glad now, because I didn't learn a lot of religious unbelief.

I do remember watching Oral Roberts on television with my grandmother. "He pays those people to say they're healed," she said.

I looked at that television wondering, *How much? $5 $10?*

I'll never forget the day, years later, when I learned a price *had* been paid for those healings.

The highest price of all.

But Oral Roberts didn't pay it.

Jesus did.

G l o r i a

Psalm 145:8-9 says, *"The Lord is gracious, and full of compassion; slow to anger, and of great mercy. The Lord is good to all: and his tender mercies are over all his works."*

Every time I read that scripture I think about my granddaddy. We called him "Pop." He was always so good to us kids. He was disposed to show favors.

When I was a little girl, I spent all my summers in the country with my grandparents. Pop would let me do anything. He let me drive his pickup when I didn't even have a driver's license.

He was good all the time. I never remember him being out of sorts or unkind to anybody. Whatever he had, he would give it to us.

Every time I think about good, I think about Pop. He was good, kind and unselfish.

That's the way God is. He's benevolent. He's full of tender mercy.

It's easy to get God to move in our lives. His tender mercies are over all His works.

Aren't you grateful? I sure am!

Gloria

I had no idea about the things of God when I was growing up. I didn't know anything about the devil either. During my school years, I was a cheerleader. In high school, our team was the Red Devils.

I cheered and cheered for the Red Devils. There was a picture of the devil's head on all our uniforms, sweaters, jackets, class rings and albums. I never thought a thing in the world about it. Except, I thought it was a pretty good name.

I learned to cheer back then, but now I've switched teams.

Today, I'm cheering for *Jesus!*

G l o r i a

Our Meeting clippings-notes remembrances

Mother & Daddy introduced me to Kenneth Sunday, October 8, 1961. They told me that they wanted me to met Dave Gardner and that he had been the life of the party at Ruby's the night before. Also that he was to call & take us airplane riding. His friend called & we met them in the penthouse at National Old Line.

They had talked about him all morning & I was convinced that this boy must be something & said so. Daddy said, "Well, we don't expect you to marry him or anything, I just think you would get a kick out of meeting him." I did.

I was not interested in Daddy's friends.

"I don't want you to marry him. I just want you to meet him," he insisted.

"We're taking him to the airport tomorrow morning," Daddy said, "just go with us to the airport." I agreed to go, and the next day we went to pick Ken and his father up from the insurance company's penthouse where they were staying.

When Ken came to the door, I noticed that there was light all around him, and I assumed that he was standing in front of a window. While everyone else talked, Ken took me out to the terrace and showed me the view of the city. He was very romantic, and endeavored to sweep me off my feet.

When we arrived at the airport, Ken took us all for a ride in an airplane, which was a big deal for me. I'd never met him before that morning, but when he left I patted him on the back, and talked to him like I'd known him forever. I didn't spend much time thinking about him after that, because I was busy at college and my life was full. Then, about two months later, I was home for the weekend and my parents decided to go to Little Rock. They invited me to join them.

"No," I said, "I'd rather stay here."

It was the strangest thing. I had a knowing that the guy I'd met in Little Rock was going to call me that weekend, and I wanted to be home for the call. I hadn't heard a word from him in two months. I had no reason to think I'd

I was so particular about the boys I dated in college, that the girls in my dorm used to tease me about it. The young men were nice enough, I just didn't like any of them in a special way. On one particular weekend, I had a date to go to a University of Arkansas ballgame in Little Rock. My parents had a function to attend in Little Rock, so they met me there for the weekend. That night I went to the game, and they went to their party. The next morning Daddy said, "I have somebody I want you to meet. He's an entertainer, he's had a gold record, and he's a pilot. He was the life of the party last night."

hear from him again, but I knew he was going to call. Sure enough, he did.

He came over and took me out on our first date. Here I was just a kid (19), and he was a mature man of the world (25), but do you know what happened? On the front porch of our house, just before I said "Good night," he proposed!

The only thing more shocking than that was when I heard myself say, "Yes." *Why did I say that?* I wondered. I didn't even know this guy. Besides, I didn't want to get married! *Well,* I thought, *I'll get out of this later.*

Thirty-five years have come and gone, and I've never tried to get out!

When I got back to the dorm after our first date, the girls gathered around and asked, "Well, did you like him?"

"Yeah," I said, "I did."

They were astonished that I'd found someone I actually liked. Ken and I started seeing each other every weekend. He had just started work at an airport only about 40 miles from my school. He would fly his old, rickety airplane over and buzz the dorm, and I would go meet him at the airport. All the girls were really impressed.

The next semester I quit school, moved to Little Rock and got a job. I lived with my grandmother. Ken moved to Little Rock and went to work until we were married at his boss's home less than six months after our first date. He borrowed $100 and took me all the way

to Hot Springs, Arkansas, 53 miles away.

Years later, I was back at that penthouse in Little Rock where I'd first met Ken. While I was there, I noticed the strangest thing. There wasn't a window that could have caused the light I'd seen around him. In fact, there was no source of light that explained that glow. Ken later told me that there was a light around me when he opened the door. I've wondered many times over the years if it was a sign from God. There's certainly no question that when Ken and I married, we began a journey that led us both to the Light of the world.

Gloria

Wallace and Mary Neece, Gloria's parents

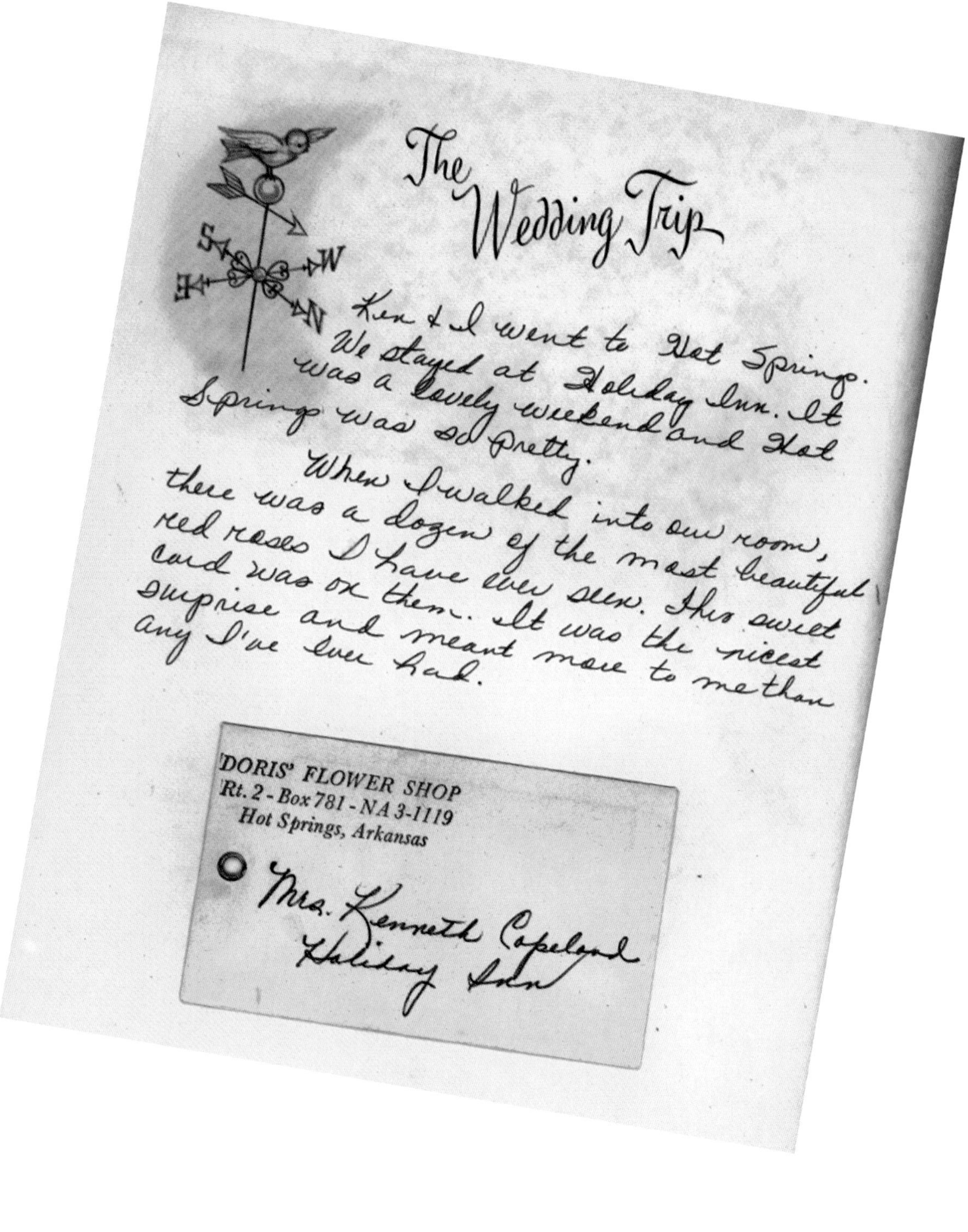

The Wedding Trip

Ken & I went to Hot Springs. We stayed at Holiday Inn. It was a lovely weekend and Hot Spring was so Pretty.

When I walked into our room, there was a dozen of the most beautiful red roses I have ever seen. This sweet card was on them. It was the nicest surprise and meant more to me than any I've ever had.

'DORIS' FLOWER SHOP
Rt. 2 - Box 781 - NA 3-1119
Hot Springs, Arkansas

Mrs. Kenneth Copeland
Holiday Inn

I fought deep, dark depression for years before I was born again. The oppression finally became so heavy that I had no emotional response to anyone in my life. I didn't have any expression of love toward anyone. Not even toward my parents! There was nobody on the face of the earth that I had any emotional feeling for.

I was mad at the world, and mad at my parents. I didn't want them coming around. I didn't want *anyone* hanging around. Now, if someone wanted to brag on me, I'd tolerate them for a while. But the first time they crossed me—they were history.

Don't misunderstand, I told people I loved them. But it was a con. I might tell a woman I loved her, but I would *never* sing to one. I could stand up on a stage and sing to a crowd, but the thought of singing to a woman was beyond me.

Why?

Because it was an expression of love.

Back then I honestly believed that there was no such thing as real love. In fact, just a few days before I met Gloria I said to someone, "I really don't believe love is a real thing. I think it's just some kind of state of mind. And if it *is* real, then I'm incapable of it."

There's no such thing as a human being incapable of love. That's a spiritual impossibility, but I didn't know it.

A few days later, I met Gloria and fell in love with her the minute I saw her.

This is different! I realized.

Every idea I'd ever had about love flew out the window.

On my first date with Gloria I found myself *singing* to her.

Whooh! Man, this is something, I thought when I caught myself. I hadn't planned on singing. I wasn't trying to impress her or con her into something. I just couldn't help it. I knew right then that I wanted to marry this woman. I figured it would take me a year to talk her into it, so I decided to get an early start. I didn't know what it would take to get her to marry me, but I was ready to lie, cheat, steal or con to make it happen.

I really thought, *This is going to take a long time—maybe years—to win her over, so I'm going to ask her now.*

After our date, I walked her up to the front porch and opened the door.

"Gloria," I said. She turned around and looked at me. "Will you marry me?"

She said, "Yes—I will." Then she turned around and went inside the house and closed the door.

Left me standing there stammering and muttering in disbelief.

God opened the door of my heart with love.

When I opened my heart enough for Gloria, Jesus came knocking. Sure enough, not too long after that, I let Him in.

Kenneth

CHAPTER 2

The Day of Salvation

The Lord is not slack concerning his promise, as some men count slackness;

but is longsuffering to us–ward, not willing that any should perish,

but that all should come to repentance. 2 PETER 3:9

I always said I'd never marry a preacher, and I didn't—I married a commercial pilot. As Ken says, we were both as lost as a goose in a fog, but we had big plans and high hopes about our future. We'd been married for about four months when we had the opportunity to go into business with some people. Ken had already gone to work for them, and we were so sure it was a sweet deal that I quit my job and went to work for them, too. Believing that we'd get rich quick, we moved out of our apartment and into a house in a fairly nice part of town.

We couldn't afford to buy it, but we managed a lease-purchase agreement.

For furniture, we had a stunning metal coffee table that Ken had made in high school shop, and a black-and-white television with a picture about one inch high—just a line through the middle! We rented a rollaway bed for $7.50 a month, and I borrowed a couple of lawn chairs from my mother.

That was it. We had no stove and no refrigerator. We didn't expect to live that way very long. We thought it would be temporary, and that soon we'd have lots of money to buy new furniture for the house.

(Facing page) Kenneth and Gloria, still newlyweds, 1962.

We were wrong. The business went broke in a few weeks. Actually, it started out that way and we didn't know it. Instead of getting rich quick, we became destitute in a hurry.

Our situation just got worse day after day. Ken's salary was gone. My salary was gone. Someone else had my old job. Our food was dwindling, and our bills were accumulating. In cold weather, I put food outside in a cardboard box. Ken's mom gave us potatoes, and I cooked them in the coffeepot. I'll never forget the day a woman came to my door. She looked around and said, "Hasn't your furniture arrived yet?"

"Not yet," I said. "It sure hasn't."

With each passing day, I felt more desperate. The only good thing about our situation was how quickly I could clean house. I had no furniture to dust, nothing to clean, nothing to eat except potatoes, and the television ceased to be a pleasure.

I had never felt that desperate in my life. No matter where I looked, I couldn't seem to find a way out. Simply stated, my world had crumbled. I was so miserable, I picked up the Bible that Vinita sent Ken for his birthday. It was a *New English Bible,* and I'd never seen one before. In the front she'd written, "Ken, precious, seek ye first the kingdom of God and His righteousness, and all these other things will be added unto you. Matthew 6:33."

Wow, I thought, *this sounds like a winner. All those other things are what we need. We don't need a few things. We need all of them!* I found that verse in the Bible and began to read. What I read just stunned me. For the first time in my life I found out that God loved me.

Until that day, I had no revelation about God. I believed in Him. I was raised in a church that had no reality of God's moving in your life on earth. They told us you wouldn't know if you were going to heaven until after you died—and you probably wouldn't make it. I wasn't born

The Wedding Gown

I wore a lovely white suit made by mother and a little white whisp hat. And a beautiful white orchid givin to me by Ken.

again, and didn't know that I needed to be. If I had known that I needed salvation, I wouldn't have had the foggiest notion about how to get it.

I'd never even heard the Good News, so when I picked up that Bible and started reading, it was the best news I'd ever heard about God. According to the Bible, God loved me and cared for me! It just seemed right to me that if He cared for birds, He cared for me! When I realized that God loved me, I just naturally responded to Him.

As I remember, I said something like, "Lord, I'm just giving You my life. Take my life and do something with it."

I didn't know when I said those simple words that I'd just changed my allegiance from the kingdom of darkness to the kingdom of God. I didn't know my spirit had been quickened with God's own life. I didn't know that I was a new

Kenneth and Gloria were married April 13, 1962.

creature. Over the next few days and weeks, I discovered a new hunger inside me for the things of God. I wanted to read the Bible. I wanted to attend church. When I finally understood what had happened, I was even more in awe. I had been born again!

G l o r i a

By the time I married Gloria, I had run from God so far, and so long, that I'd run myself into a dead end. I knew I was called to preach, but just the mention of God scared me so badly, I'd run in any direction. Gloria and I didn't have much to start with when we got married, and in less than a month I managed to lose everything we had. I mean, I wiped us out. Afterward, I was out desperately trying to find work, checking out all the flight schools, trying to find a job flying airplanes. Gloria was at home in a mess. The only thing she had to cook in was a coffeepot! We were using the coffee table I made in high school shop class. If there was ever a time in my life when I was scared out of my wits, that was the time.

One day during that period, I sat down in the living room to put on my shoes. Suddenly, I heard the voice of the Holy Spirit, *If you and your family don't get in line with the Word of God, you'll go to the devil's hell.*

I dropped my shoe. There wasn't anywhere left to run. There wasn't anywhere to hide.

"I know it, Lord! I know it!" I cried. "I'll do whatever I have to do. Now, what do I do?"

It was as though the Holy Spirit punched a rewind button in my memory. Suddenly I heard the distinctly familiar voice of my childhood Sunday school teacher, Mrs. Taggart. "Boys," she said, "you have to ask Jesus into your heart."

I didn't wait another second. I cried out for Jesus to move in!

That day, sitting alone in my living room, one of the greatest miracles since the dawn of time took place. It was a greater miracle than creation. It was a greater miracle than cancers disappearing or limbs growing out again. It was a greater miracle than turning water into wine. Greater even than raising the dead. Until Jesus splits the sky on His return, there will never be a greater miracle than the rebirth of a human spirit.

For 20 years, my life had been a mess, but at that moment, 1962 in North Little Rock, Arkansas, I stopped trying to hide that mess from God. Instead, I walked up and handed it to Him! He took it and by His grace I was never the same again.

K e n n e t h

The night I received the Baptism in the Holy Ghost, I didn't have the faintest notion what I was doing. I hadn't been saved very long when my folks took Gloria and me to a meeting in East Texas. I sat there thinking, *Whew, I'm only here by the skin of my teeth! I almost went to hell!* I didn't want to hold out on God anymore. If somebody had said, "The Lord is sending someone to the moon and back tonight, who wants to go?" I would have volunteered. I just didn't want to miss anything.

Toward the end of the meeting, they gave an invitation for people to come forward and receive the Holy Spirit. I'd read a few things about that, but I hadn't understood anything I read. Mama and Daddy were sitting behind us, so I turned around to Mama. "Is that something we ought to have?"

"You ought to have it," she said, nodding.

I came up out of that seat and charged down front. About the time I reached the altar, a bunch of men got on me, and a bunch of women gathered

around Gloria. I'd never heard people pray like that. To tell the truth, I was a little shocked when they jumped me.

"Let go! Let go, and let God!" one of them hollered.

"Hang on, Brother! Hang on!" another shouted.

I didn't know how to do either one, so I just stood there. Well, nothing happened to me, so they finally quit. About then, a bold friend of mine said, "Let's go over there and pray for Gloria." The women were still whooping over her when I stepped up from behind. I didn't know what to pray, so I just said, "Lord, give her the Holy Spirit."

My friend said, "Lay your hand on her."

"No," I said, "I'm not going to lay my hands on anybody and pray." I thought, *Are you kidding? We don't do that!*

"Lay your hand on her," he repeated.
"No."
"Lay your hand on her."
"No!"
"LAY YOUR HAND ON HER!"

I reached out and touched her back. Woomp! It felt like 800 volts of electricity went up through my arm. I don't remember giving Gloria another thought because at that moment, the power of God hit me! I kind of staggered over to a chair and sat down. Something was happening to me! Something started moving around in the bottom of my belly.

"Oh, Lord, Oh, Jesus," I said.

"Oh, Jesus!"

My friend touched me on the head and said, "Don't speak in English."

I didn't even think, I just opened my mouth and started praying in an unknown tongue. I prayed, and prayed, and prayed.

I'd never heard the word anointing. I didn't even know that Jesus was the One Who baptized in the Holy Spirit. I didn't know that John had said, "There's One coming after me Who will baptize you with the Holy Ghost, and with fire!" (See Matthew 3:11.) But I received nevertheless.

Gloria (who still didn't even know she had been born again) received the Holy Ghost the next night. Finally, we were both saved and filled with the Holy Ghost. But five long years passed before we really understood what we had.

Kenneth

Ken was always quicker to act on things than I was. So when A.W. and Vinita took us to that meeting down in Nacogdoches, Texas, where we found out about the Baptism in the Holy Ghost, Ken was ready and raring to receive it. I was a little more reluctant. Even by today's standards, that meeting was pretty wild. I'd never heard anyone

speak in tongues, and I didn't know anything about it. Ken received the Holy Spirit during one of the first services, but I didn't. I still wasn't sure about it. The next day, I sat in the meeting wondering, *Is this of God or not?* You have to remember, I didn't know anything. Until a short time before, I wasn't even sure God existed.

Well, I thought, *I just think I'll go upstairs, have a cigarette and pray about this.*

That's exactly what I did. I went upstairs, lit up a cigarette and said, "Lord, I don't know if this Holy Spirit is of You or not, but if it is, well, I'll take it." Can you believe that? How dense can you be! It didn't bother me to smoke, but I sure wanted to be careful about receiving the Baptism in the Holy Ghost!

You can probably guess what happened at the next meeting. The Holy Spirit met me right where I was, cigarettes and all. He filled me to overflowing with Himself. This just proves you don't have to know much to receive the Holy Spirit. When you are ready, He is ready. Pretty soon, those cigarettes were gone forever. I didn't need to smoke. I was lit up with the fire of God.

Gloria

"I always said I'd never marry a preacher, and I didn't—I married a commercial pilot."

— GLORIA

Gloria, Kenneth,
John and Kellie,
Fort Worth, Texas,
1968.

Ken and I came back to Little Rock, after receiving the Baptism in the Holy Spirit, with a desire to do something for the Lord. But we had no idea what to do. We didn't have any teaching and didn't even realize we needed any. We wanted to live a godly life, but we didn't know how. So we lived like everyone else.

Although we had moved into an apartment with furniture, we continued to have tremendous financial problems. Nothing worked out for us. For about five years, either we didn't get the money out of a job we'd done, or something would happen and the job would fall through. *The Amplified Bible* hadn't been out very long, and my friend Suzanne Best and I started reading it. Then we started getting together with another lady every week to study and pray. We didn't have any teaching, and we didn't know much about prayer, but we did one thing right. We believed what we read on the pages of that Bible.

God ministered to us and taught us some things, but we didn't know enough to live in victory. Our lives were ruled by our circumstances.

After a while, Ken and I moved to Fort Worth. Ken worked selling insurance with his dad. He was miserable doing it because he still wasn't doing what God had called him to do.

Looking back over those five years, I suspect nobody would have picked us out of a crowd and charged us with being Christians. Yet, those were the years when I learned to put the Word in my heart. I took what I read there literally. Although it wasn't often apparent on the outside, the Word of God was creating a stability in me. It anchored my soul.

G l o r i a

After Ken and I got saved and filled with the Holy Spirit, my grandmother wanted us to pray for her so she'd get healed. The problem was that she'd been steeped in years of religious unbelief.

"Now, Mom," I'd say, "I'm going to pray for you. *That's* when you believe you receive your healing."

I'd pray for her. Afterward, I'd tell her to say, "Thank You, Jesus, for healing me."

She'd say that.

"Now," I said, "say, 'I now believe I receive my healing.'"

"'Thank You, Jesus, for healing me.'"

She *wouldn't* say she believed she received.

One day I was working with her, trying to get her to say she believed she received. Each time, she said something different.

Finally, she looked at me in exasperation. "Gloria, you *can't fool Jesus!*"

I laugh every time I think about that. She was right, of course. You can't fool Jesus.

What my grandmother (and all the rest of us) need to learn is that when we believe the symptoms of sickness and disease instead of believing the Word of God that says by Jesus' stripes *"ye were healed"* (1 Peter 2:24), we're not fooling Jesus. We're letting the devil fool *us!*

Gloria

Gloria's grandparents —"Mom" and "Pop," Alger and Clara Neece.

Back when I first got saved and filled with the Holy Spirit, I read in the Bible that the only way to please God was through faith. Since I'd spent literally years of my life displeasing God, living by faith seemed like a good idea to me. I thought, *There's a Hall of Fame here in Hebrews 11. Every one of those people lived by faith. I believe that's what I'll do.*

So I'd go to someone I considered to be a spiritual person and ask, "How do you live by faith?"

"Well, now, you'd better watch out!" said one fellow.

"Huh?"

"You'd better use some wisdom!" said another.

"I don't have any!" I said. "All I've ever known is sin. That's why I want to learn how to live by faith."

I'd go to church and hear, "You ought to live by faith!"

"OK!" I told Gloria. "We'll go back next Sunday, and they'll surely tell us how."

The next Sunday's message was on "What Will Happen If You Have Faith!"

"We're getting close! Next Sunday they'll tell us how to do it."

The following Sunday the preacher would tell us, "What Will Happen If You Don't Have Faith!"

I'd be so excited. I'd think, *I'm learning! I found out I ought to have faith. I found out what will happen if I don't have faith. Now I know what will happen if I have faith. Surely next Sunday they'll tell me how to live by faith.*

The next week they preached on Paul's thorn in the flesh.

The week after, they preached on Job.

The next week they'd say, "You ought to live by faith."

I wanted to stand up and holler, "How do you do it?"

When I asked questions, nobody answered me.

"How are you, Brother Copeland?"

"Fine," I'd say. "Let me ask you a question. How do you live by faith?"

I never got a straight answer.

It never occurred to me that they didn't know. I thought maybe God was holding out on me because of the way I'd lived before I was saved. *Maybe God is still mad,* I'd think, *and He doesn't want me to have any faith.*

That can't be right! I'd argue. *The Bible says there's no way to please God without faith. Surely, after all these years, He wants me to please Him!*

Those questions gnawed at me for five years. They were gnawing at me when I went to bed, and they were still gnawing at me when I woke up. The Lord kept telling me I was to minister the gospel, but I knew I couldn't do that. "Dear God, You know how I lived before I got saved!" When I asked God how to live by faith, it seemed to me He was telling me to go to Oral Roberts University.

"I can't do that," I said. "How could I go to college, hold down a job, and support my wife and our small children?" It was impossible. *Besides,* I thought, *I was a dummy when I was in school. I can't be any smarter now than I was then. I'm about to turn 30 years old, and I don't have any raging desire to go somewhere and flunk!*

Five years after I'd been saved and filled with the Holy Spirit, I still didn't know how to please God through faith, and I still hadn't gone to ORU.

Gloria and I were talking one day and I said, "There's just no way for me to go to Oral Roberts University. We have all these bills, and the children! We'd starve!"

God put wisdom in Gloria's mouth, because the words she spoke changed the course of our lives. "Kenneth, we're starving now," she said. "Wouldn't it be better to starve in the will of God, than starve out of the will of God?"

I just looked at her.

She was right!

God had been telling me how to go to ORU for five years! He wanted me to go by faith!

K e n n e t h

CHAPTER 3

Oral Roberts University

The fear of the Lord is the beginning of wisdom; a good understanding have all those who do His commandments; His praise endures forever. PSALM 111:10

The first thing we did about possibly attending ORU was go up there with my mother and dad for a seminar. We'd been in the seminar for several days, and during the closing service, Brother Roberts invited everyone in the congregation to join the prayer line so he could lay hands on them. I got in the line ahead of Gloria and my parents, so after Brother Roberts laid his hands on me and prayed, I took a seat toward the front to wait. I wasn't paying a lot of attention to what was going on. I was just basking in the anointing, which was very strong. While I sat there, God opened my eyes to a realm of the spirit I'd never seen before. The scene before me was so staggering that I shut my eyes. A few minutes later, I opened them again and the vision was still there. It really hit me hard.

It was as though the people in that line were transparent. I could see a vague outline of each person's body. Most of them were healthy people. But I clearly saw the spirit man inside each person. There wasn't a healthy spirit in the bunch! They looked so scrawny and sickly that they could hardly walk. Yet, on top of each emaciated, little spirit body was a huge head. It literally broke my heart. I cried

(Facing page)
The prayer tower at Oral Roberts University, Tulsa, Oklahoma.

and wept until finally I could hardly stand the sight. "Lord," I cried, "what is this?"

Son, He answered, *I have called you to feed My people. They are out of balance. They are physically developed. They're mentally developed. Some are so developed mentally that they can hardly hold their head up. I'll show you how to feed My people and build them up spiritually until they become balanced.*

During the next few days, every time I'd try to talk to Gloria about what I'd seen, I just wept. Even today, all these years later, it still hurts my heart when I think about that sight. It still moves me to obey the command Jesus gave in John 21:17—"*Feed my sheep.*"

The Lord told me to go to Oral Roberts University in 1963, but it took me until December of 1966 to obey Him. When we finally packed up and moved to Tulsa, I realized that I was in the will of God for the first time in my life. Until then my disobedience to God had cost me the joy of my salvation. It had cost me the peace of God. It had cost me the fulfillment of knowing I was doing exactly what God set me on earth to do. I was almost 30 years old, and in all my adult life, I'd never experienced a full day of God's will. By the time we got to Tulsa, I didn't care if we ever had anything or not! I was beside myself with joy!

For the first time in my life, I was truly satisfied.

Kenneth

Rufus Moseley, a great man of prayer, used to tell about a time when he lay in a Chicago hotel room crying out to God...and crying out to God...and crying out to God. All of a sudden he thought, *Here lies a fool who knows nothing, doing all the talking to Somebody Who knows everything!*

That pretty much sums up my prayer life when Gloria and I moved to Tulsa. I needed money to pay my tuition. I needed money to buy books. I needed money to support my family. And I was desperately crying out to God about it!

Here was my dilemma: I knew that most likely within a week I could land a job as a pilot and get some money coming in, but every time I'd start hunting a job, my insides would just fold up. I didn't know what to do. I had to have a job. But if I was off flying somewhere, when would I go to school?

"I'm supposed to register for school in a couple of days," I told Gloria, "and I don't know what to do. So, I'm going into that room, and I'm going to lock the door. I'm not coming out until I hear from God, even if it takes a month!"

I went in there and slammed the door. I fell down on my face on the floor and started praying as hard as I could. I realize now that 99 percent of it was unbelief, but it was honest unbelief. I just didn't know any better. Suddenly, a thought crossed my mind. *I wonder what would happen if I would just be quiet? I wonder if God would answer me?*

I got still and quiet, and inside my spirit I heard the Lord say, *It's about time! I haven't been able to get a word in edgewise. Stand up on your feet! Don't you know how to come to attention?*

I jumped to my feet. Every hair on the back of my neck stood at attention.

"Was God's voice audible?" you might ask.

It was to me! It was so audible that even my toes heard it. I doubt anyone else would have heard it if they had been standing there, but every cell in my body heard it. Every bone heard it. My nose heard what God said that day.

I sent you here to go to school, and I'll take care of you, He said. *You go take a full load of classes.*

"What about a job?" I asked.

Silence.

"Yes, Lord," I said, "thank You." Gloria was surprised when I walked out. "A month!" she said. "You haven't been in there for 20 minutes!" The problem hadn't been my getting God's attention. The difficulty had been in God's getting mine.

Kenneth

The day arrived when I had to enroll in school—that meant paying for tuition and books—and I didn't have a dime. In fact, I don't know why we even had a checking account back then. We didn't have any money to write a check. Still, God had said that He would take care of me, so I drove to the campus hoping for a miracle.

When I got there, I didn't see any evidence of one. After registering for classes, I took my place in the back of the long line at the registrar's office with no clue how to pay that bill. "God, You said You'd take care of me," I prayed, watching the line get shorter and shorter. Two or three times, I thought about calling my dad, because he was the only one who would accept a collect call from me. I resisted the urge.

Finally, it was my turn. I completed the registration, and Mrs. Campbell started typing the bill. *What am I going to do?*

"Mrs. Campbell, may I use your phone?"

The expansive campus of Oral Roberts University.

"Certainly," she said.

"Daddy?" I asked when the collect call went through.

"Kenneth! Where in the world are you?"

"I'm at the registrar's office enrolling in school."

"Well, I've been trying to find you," Dad said. "A fellow came by my office yesterday and gave me some money to put in your ministry. I figured you'd need it quick, so I took it to the bank and deposited it in your account."

God put money in my account yesterday!

"Daddy," I asked, looking over at the bill Mrs. Campbell was typing, "how much did you put in there?"

He told me. I did some fast figuring. After I paid my tithe, there would be enough for my first-quarter tuition, my books and all my fees—with a dime left over.

I hung up the telephone, and wrote the check.

When God tells you He'll take care of something, He'll do what He said. You can take it to the bank.

Kenneth

hen I walked out of that registrar's office with my bill paid, I felt like a faith giant. I thought I could do anything. That is, until I started out the door and heard the Lord say, *Go to the top floor.*

I stopped in my tracks. I'd already been around ORU long enough to know that students weren't allowed on the top floor. I turned and walked back to the elevator. Inside, I pressed the button for the fifth floor, not the sixth. I reasoned to myself that I was obeying God by going to the top floor that allowed students.

When the elevator door opened, there was nothing there. Not even a chair. "Well, thank God my tuition is paid," I said, stepping back on the elevator.

I said to go to the top floor!

"Lord, that's like the Vatican! That's where Brother Roberts' office is. They don't let us go up there!"

You do what I tell you. They work for Me.

I pressed the button for the top floor. A minute later, I stepped off the elevator right in the middle of the executive offices. I knew I wasn't supposed to be there. Worse, I didn't have any idea what God wanted me to do. When the receptionist, Ruth Rooks, looked up at me, I just blurted the first thing that came to my mind.

"Uh...my name is Kenneth Copeland. I'm a commercial pilot, and I've just enrolled in school. I know this is a traveling ministry, so I just wanted somebody to know that I'm a qualified, commercial pilot. If anyone needs anything like that, I sure do need work. Thank you. God bless you."

"Tell him," she said, nodding to a man who'd come out of an office.

So I told him.

"I don't know of a thing," he said, shaking his head.

"Thank you very much," I said, feeling like an idiot. "'Bye." I turned to leave, and ran head-on into Oral Roberts himself!

Now Brother Roberts is a big man—over 6 feet tall. But at that moment when

I looked up at him, he looked even bigger than that. He seemed at least 8 feet tall. "My name is Oral Roberts," he said, offering his hand.

I said something brilliant like, "Hum-a-hum-hum-a!"

"Did I hear you say you're a commercial pilot?" he asked.

"Yes, sir."

"Can you handle our airplane?"

"Yes, sir. I can."

"Two weeks ago we started to hire a co-pilot for the evangelistic team's airplane," he said, "but the Lord told me not to do it. He said there was a student coming that He wanted to have the job. You're my man."

I shuddered to think about how close I'd come to messing up. I could have barreled ahead and gotten some other kind of job. God wouldn't have bothered me about it at all. He would have let me take care of myself.

God was clearly giving me a choice. I could live by my wits, or I could live by faith. I hadn't even attended my first class at ORU. What an education!

The Lord told me to take a full-course load in school, and that's just what I did. I took a full schedule, including algebra. On the first day of my algebra class, the professor began by saying, "Good morning, everyone." I remember those words well, because they were the last ones that professor said that I ever understood.

I'll never forget what it was like to study for that course. I hadn't been in school in 13 years, and my brain cramped every five minutes. Seriously! It would just seize up and I wouldn't be able to think anything. At those times I couldn't even think of my name. But the Holy Ghost helped me and I soon found out if I prayed in other tongues for a few minutes, my mind would loosen up and I could think again. The more I prayed in the Spirit, the longer I could study. Learning that helped me even more than the algebra did.

Kenneth

I hadn't been at Oral Roberts University long when my mother gave us a tape of Kenneth E. Hagin preaching on Mark 11:23-24. When I heard that tape, I finally realized the Bible was actually true! Of course, if you'd asked me if I thought it was true before that time, I would have said yes. But I didn't know you could believe it and act on it, and it would come to pass. I didn't know it was literally God speaking to me.

That first tape of Brother Hagin's turned me on so much, I immediately got all of his tapes that I could get my hands on. I turned on those tapes and turned off everything else in my life. I turned off the television. I turned off the radio. I threw away the newspaper. I told Gloria that I just had to get full of the Word. I wanted to be overflowing with the Word. I got up in the morning, and before I did anything else, I leaned over and started that tape player. I shaved with the Word. I dressed with the Word. I ate with the Word. I even started taking my reel-to-reel tape recorder with me in the car. Day and night, I put the Word in my heart, until my spirit was full. Our circumstances didn't look any better. We still lived in a dumpy rent house. Every house after mine, all the way to the end of the block, was condemned and torn down. (That tells you something about the neighborhood where we lived.) But I began to have an insight that God created me in the likeness of Jesus because He wanted to fellowship with me. He wanted to run with me, and raise me up. He wanted to enjoy me and let me enjoy Him. I found out that God would do anything in the world for me. In fact, He already had—on the Cross.

Do you know what happened?

I fell in love with God!

It isn't that I hadn't loved God before then. I had, but I'd never fallen in love with Him. There is a difference.

I was driving down the road one afternoon when that love started welling up from inside me, and I had to pull the car over and stop. It was the first time in my life I ever came to God without begging Him for something.

"Father, I can't drive this car because I love You so much I need to hold my hands up and tell You about it," I said. "I just want to tell You how much I love You, and how much I care for You. I worship You! I'm not here because I need something from You. All my needs are met. I just want to love You."

That old, worn-out car was leaking from every joint, but when I fell in love with God, I stopped worrying about that car or anything else. I just knew that in Him I had all that I'd ever need.

Kenneth

Looking back, I see how the Lord began teaching me in those years I traveled with Brother Roberts how vitally important it is to protect the anointing. To be perfectly honest, at the time I didn't even know what the anointing was. I thought it was goose bumps. I heard Christians say, "My, wasn't that anointed tonight?"

No, I'd think, *it wasn't anointed. I didn't get one goose bump.* That's all I knew.

That's all most people knew.

On my first trip with Brother Roberts, my boss said, "I need you to drive Brother Roberts' car."

"OK, what do you want me to do?"

"I want you to keep your mouth shut. Never speak, for any reason, unless you're spoken to."

I didn't think that would be much of a problem, because I couldn't think of anything to say to him anyway. I drove him around in total silence, and that

"When I touched a person, off my faith went to God. I was never aware that Kenneth was study-ing me." —*Dr. Oral Roberts referring to the time Kenneth was a student at ORU in the late '60s.*

very first day I realized that he was protecting something.

A lot of people thought he was unsociable. If the only time you ever saw him was when he was ministering, or preparing to minister, I can understand why you might think so. But if you saw him any other time, he was friendly and interested in visiting with people.

The first meeting I drove for him was in Bluefield, West Virginia. After we landed, I drove him to the hotel, then I went back to the airport to take care of the airplane. When I finished, I drove back to the hotel and went to the restaurant to eat. While I was eating, I saw Mrs. Roberts come in and sit down. A few minutes later, Brother Roberts came in and sat at a different table!

They're fussing! I thought.

Then I saw them look at one another, smile and wave. They grinned, and acted very happy to see each other!

That's the strangest thing I've ever seen. Those people are peculiar!

That night at the service, there was a young man in the prayer line who was totally paralyzed. They brought him up there, and Brother Roberts laid hands on him. The power of God was so strong, it crackled like little bolts of lightning when he touched him. Instantly healed, the guy jumped up and ran across the platform!

During the second service, a woman came to the healing line holding her crippled son. His little legs looked like two loose ropes just hanging there. When Brother Roberts put his hands on that boy, he started kicking.

"Put me down, Mama! Put me down!" he cried.

"No, no, no!" she said, but he kicked loose and took off running. The anointing hit that entire auditorium and everyone leapt to their feet, shouted and praised God.

In time, I learned that when he was ministering, Brother Roberts wouldn't visit with anybody after 2 o'clock in the afternoon. For some reason, that particular night the anointing was so strong, that to protect it, he didn't even visit with his wife.

"Wasn't that going a little bit too far?" someone asked me once.

That man and little boy who received their miracles didn't think so.

The Lord made sure my first lesson in ministry was to protect the anointing. Why? Because the anointing is the power of God to destroy yokes of bondage. I learned that you can preach the most perfect sermon in the world, but if there is no anointing, there will be no miracles. The anointing means the Anointed One and His Anointing. That's Jesus. If you want the anointing to destroy yokes, develop a relationship with Him. Then, protect it.

Kenneth

I'll never forget the first time I ever walked into an auditorium full of invalids waiting to be healed. It was in 1967 in Memphis, Tennessee. I'd helped fly Brother Roberts to his meeting there, and I decided to go over to the meeting hall a little early and look around.

When I stepped inside, cold chills ran up and down my spine. That building was full of the sickest bunch of people I had ever seen in my life. The sick, the poor, the lame, the deaf, the blind, the mentally ill—they were all there— hundreds of them! I will never forget the smell of sickness, disease and death that assaulted me when I walked inside.

Back then, those kinds of people were swept under the social rug. I had never seen anything like it and it scared me—bad! I took one look around and thought, *Nope, this isn't for me. I'm in the wrong place.*

I turned around and walked out the side door of that auditorium, talking to God under my breath. "I'm going home right now," I said. "I'm going to get on a Greyhound bus, and I'm headed back for Tulsa. Oral Roberts can figure out how to get that airplane back to Tulsa by himself." I had never seen such a frightful sight in my life. It just turned my insides upside down. By the time I got outside, I was talking to God out loud. "I'm through! Do you understand that? Oral Roberts or no Oral Roberts, I'm going home! I don't care what I have to do— anything is better than this."

At that moment, something totally unexpected happened to me. My feet

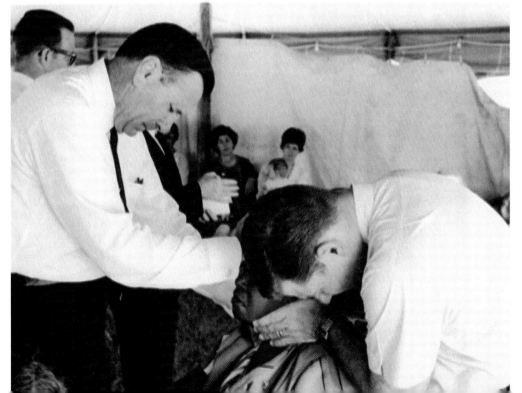

Brother Roberts' ministry set up invalid tents like this during their meetings for people too sick to be in the main tent. It was here that Kenneth learned to pray for the sick to be made whole.

stuck to the sidewalk. I couldn't move! I knew pretty quickly that God had something to say to me.

I looked up. "Let me loose!"

He didn't.

My insides were raging. I'd never been gripped in such fear. By now, I wasn't talking quietly. I was yelling. "Let me go! I don't have anything to give those people in there!"

God answered me. *I know you don't! But I do! That's why I baptized you in My Spirit.*

As soon as He said that, my feet turned loose.

I had a choice. The strange thing was that all of a sudden I wanted to go back in there. I retraced my steps and made myself go back. That night I carefully watched the way Brother Roberts ministered to the people. It stirred faith in me. It stirred a healing ministry in me. The yoke of fear was so destroyed, that I never again wanted to back out on people who were desperate for God. How could I? God never backed out on me.

Kenneth

Most of the time I was responsible for the airplane and the car during those trips with Brother Roberts. After my part was finished, I helped out anyway I could. I held his coat, etc., until the service was over and then drove him back to the hotel.

One night I was told by Brother Collins Steele, Senior Manager and director of the meetings, "I want you to go to the invalid room (a set-apart room for people who were unable to manage being in the main crowd). There are loudspeakers in there so that people can hear Brother Roberts' message. Listen carefully to what he preaches, then after the invitation, you'll have a few minutes before he comes in to lay hands on them. During that time, go over the main points of the message again and get them ready."

"Yes, sir."

The "invalid room!" There were people with every disease imaginable. People who were insane. One woman there had cancer of the stomach. She couldn't have weighed more than 75 pounds. A nurse attended her, and she was so weak she couldn't even turn over without help.

During the service, I stood under the speakers and listened to Brother Roberts' every word. Afterward, I said,

"Now, remember what Brother Roberts said. You need to expect a miracle. He also wants you to make the laying on of hands your point of contact. Start saying right now, 'The moment he touches me, the power and anointing of Almighty God is going into me, and I believe I receive my healing.' Then begin to do something, if it's nothing except moving your little finger."

About then Brother Roberts walked through the door, and I stepped back. He walked in, looked around and stood there for a moment. Then, he turned and looked at me. He took one step back and grabbed me by the shoulder of my coat. "Now, you're going to do the laying on of hands."

Me? I thought. All the color drained out of my face. I'd never prayed for anything or anybody like that in my life.

"Don't be concerned about making mistakes," he said. "I'm going to be right there next to you, and I'll stop you and correct any mistakes you make. God will bless it." He also said, "Don't touch them until you're ready to release your faith."

He walked me over to the woman with cancer of the stomach.

Lord, couldn't we do this one last? I thought. *I'd like to practice around the room before we get to her.*

Her nurse lifted her over onto her side so that she could see us.

I began to pray and then had just reached out to touch her, when suddenly it sounded like the Lion of the tribe of Judah walked up behind me. Brother Roberts roared the words, "In the Name of Jesus, Whose I am and Whom I serve, you foul, unclean spirit attempting to take the life of my sister, you come out of her!"

Suddenly with a coughing, blowing kind of sound, she blew that cancer out on the floor. Just blew it out! The thing looked like a jellyfish! The next thing I knew, she had jumped off that bed. She ran around screaming, "I'm healed! I'm healed! I'm healed!"

After that, I was roaring and ready to go. "Look out, devil! Here we come."

K e n n e t h

few weeks before we moved to Tulsa, I made a commitment to God. I prayed and said, "Lord, I'll do whatever You want me to do. If You reveal it to me, I'll do it even if I don't want to."

Soon afterward, I heard Brother Roberts say that the Lord told him if he wanted greater revelation of Jesus, he should read the Gospels and Acts four times in 30 days. The Lord impressed me that that's what He wanted me to do, too.

Unfortunately, we'd just moved to Tulsa, and everything was still in boxes. I hadn't even unpacked. The place was just a mess. Our children were still small enough to need a lot of attention. I couldn't put them off for 30 minutes, much less 30 days!

Finally, I talked it over with Ken, who had just started school at ORU. "You know if I do this," I explained, "I may not be able to cook. I may not be able to keep up with the ironing. I may not be able to get this stuff unpacked until after I finish. But I feel like it's what God wants me to do. I just want to know if you'll go along with it."

He told me to do whatever I thought I should do. So I sat down and figured up how many hours it would take each day, then divided those hours into three different times. I decided that I would get up at 5:30 every morning and read until the rest of the family got up. Then, after lunch, I would put the kids down for a nap and read until they woke up. At night, I would read as long as it took to finish for the day. All totaled, I would be

The little house in Tulsa. It was here Gloria learned to put the Word first place in her life.

spending about 4½ hours reading the Bible.

The first day I followed the plan, the strangest thing happened. By 3 in the afternoon, all my work was done for the day. I was amazed. I'd spent literally hours in the Word of God, and all my work was done. That hadn't happened to me once since we'd moved to Tulsa!

By the end of the first week, I had done everything I needed to do. Boxes were unpacked. The laundry and ironing were done. The house was clean. I even antiqued four pieces of furniture from start to finish!

It took me a while to find out how that was possible. I found the answer in Proverbs 4:7-8, *"For skillful and godly Wisdom is the principle thing.... Prize Wisdom highly and exalt her, and she will exalt and promote you; she will bring you to honor when you embrace her"* *(The Amplified Bible).*

Now, 30 years later, I will catch myself feeling bogged down at times, thinking, *How am I going to get everything done?* As soon as I catch myself feeling that pressure, I say to myself, *Gloria, you haven't been spending enough time in the Word or this wouldn't be happening!*

I slow down and give the Word first place. I give the Word final authority. I prize it highly. I exalt it. Then the rest of my life moves into its rightful place.

G l o r i a

When Ken enrolled as a freshman at Oral Roberts University, he got a job as a member of the flight crew and was paid $100 a month. That $100, some money from the GI Bill and some money Ken's parents would send was our monthly income. Add it all up and it still wasn't enough. I was at home with small children, living in a house down by the river with brown paint peeling off every wall. Ken had been in debt before we married, and in addition to our rent, utilities, gas, food and car payment, we had his loans to pay. We were in desperate financial straits. We had tried to tithe. It was something we wanted to do, but as soon as we paid our tithe, we'd get behind on our bills. Our creditors would start pressuring us. We would need money to buy groceries. So, eventually we'd go back to just giving a little bit when we could.

As we learned more and more about the Word of God, we realized that tithing was a serious matter with God. We found out that there was no scriptural reason for not tithing. Finally, it dawned on us that by not tithing, we were in rebellion to God. "That's it!" we declared. "From this day forward, we're going to tithe first. God will get His 10 percent, and we'll just have to make do with what's left. If we don't have money for food, we won't eat, but we're going to pay our tithe."

Once we made the decision to tithe, and we refused to back off that stand, an amazing thing started happening. God began multiplying the 90 percent! We actually began making it from month to month on what we had. Things were still tight, and there was more we needed to learn about financial freedom, but the day we made a quality decision to tithe no matter what happened, we changed the course of our financial future.

Gloria

During those first, financially strapped months at ORU, Ken went to one of Brother Roberts' tent meetings and came home all fired up. "We're going to be partners with Oral Roberts," he said. "From now on, we're going to give him $10 a month!"

I could hardly believe my ears. "Where do you think you're going to get $10 a month?" I asked.

"I don't know," he admitted, "but that's what we're going to do."

I couldn't work up any excitement about it. We had closed down our checking account. I was the one having to pray in tongues when I went to the grocery store so I'd be able to pay for what was in my basket. Whatever I had in my purse was all I had. I didn't see how we could afford to send $10 to Brother Roberts every month, no matter how much I would have liked to bless his ministry. Besides, it was pretty clear to me that we needed the money more than he did.

"We are going to do this!" Ken said. He had made up his mind.

Out of our meager monthly income we'd been trying to stretch, we paid our tithe first, and now we added another $10 offering to Brother Roberts. The strangest thing started happening. People began to hand us $20.

Twenty dollars! That was a lot of money.

I learned through experience what Ken had learned through hearing the Word. We'd set ourselves in the position to be blessed by tithing and by becoming partners with a ministry that was spreading the gospel. Financially, we began to increase. Things began to turn around from the time we put God first with our money by giving Him the first 10 percent, just as His Word teaches. It works!

Gloria

When Ken started school at ORU, his horizons really began to expand. Not only was he studying for school, but he was traveling with Brother Roberts and attending all his meetings. He heard so much of the Word that he was thrilled and excited when he came home.

I was at home with small children, and no money. By this time, we were learning from Kenneth Hagin to put the Word first place in our lives, to believe it, to act on it and to speak it out our mouths. I was determined to get the Word of God in abundance in my heart. I was convinced this was the answer. I meditated on the Word day and night. When I found the stability of the Word of God, it seemed like I found the answer I'd been looking for. I was so excited that I devoured everything I could find. I studied the Bible, I listened to tapes and I read books. I never said, "Well, I don't think I'll watch television anymore." I just didn't have time for it. Besides, there was nothing on television as exciting as what I began to see in God's Word.

I got up every morning with the Word on my mind while I hurried through my housework, so I could spend time in the Word. I began to see that the Word could be depended on, and that what I saw in it was mine. I listened to tapes and took notes. I remember my heart being so full one day while I was hanging up clothes that when the telephone rang, I ran inside and answered it by shouting, "Hallelujah!" Sometimes Ken would phone home from some wonderful meeting and the Word would spill out of my heart. I'd just preach him a sermon on the telephone!

I kept feeding my spirit on redemption and all that Jesus had purchased for us. The excitement grew each day. I wasn't just listening to the Word. I acted on what I learned as fast as I could. Something was happening on the inside of me.

Before long, the day came when the Word I had put into my heart became big. The Word became bigger than our lack. The Word became bigger than our debt. The Word became bigger than our old car. The Word became bigger than all our circumstances. Outwardly, our circumstances hadn't changed, but I knew they would before long. Sure enough...they did!

Gloria

Ken and I had made a quality decision that we would do whatever we saw in the Word of God, but we cringed when we ran across Romans 13:8, *"Owe no man any thing, but to love."* Owe no man? We lived in debt.

I discovered soon after our wedding that I'd married Kenneth Copeland and his notes. The idea of getting out of debt was almost a joke. When I looked at all the debt we owed, I figured that Kenneth must have borrowed money on his tricycle.

We had an old car, an old house with old furniture and not many clothes. Yet we were more than $15,000 in debt. (And that was in the '60s when a dollar was worth much more than it is today!)

When we saw that verse in Romans, we were amazed. How could someone live without debt? How would we ever buy a new car? With cash? The idea seemed ludicrous. How would we ever buy a house? If we didn't borrow money, how could we ever get ahead?

We were behind on our bills. We were being threatened with lawsuits by our creditors. It looked impossible to us.

But we'd made a commitment to God, so we said, "OK, if that's what the Bible says, that's what we'll do." We immediately stopped borrowing money or charging anything. If we could pay for something, we bought it. If we didn't have the cash, we did without it. After paying our tithe and offering, we bought groceries, gas and made payments the best we could.

Some people have said we were extreme in our response to the verse "Owe no man anything." If so, I'm glad we were because I'll tell you what it did. It made us extremely dependent on God. Back then, we didn't have any revelation of prosperity. We didn't quit borrowing money to get blessed. We quit because we saw it in God's Word.

We stayed with our commitment even though it wasn't easy to do. Eleven months after we stopped borrowing money, we were completely out of debt.

"How did it happen?" you ask.

Many times during the past 30 years I've wondered the same thing. I don't know how God did it any more than I know how He fed 5,000 people with those few loaves and fishes. I don't know how He did it any more than I know how He turned water into wine.

But He did it.

When we faithfully obeyed one scripture, God broke the little that we had and blessed it. In the process, He broke the power of debt off our backs forever. That's a miracle.

G l o r i a

One thing I learned while traveling with Brother Roberts was to expect miracles. Again and again, that's what he told people to do. When they did it, the results were often astounding. One time, for example, I was with Brother Roberts in Jacksonville, Florida, and I saw a young girl in the invalid tent who was paralyzed. She'd been tied to a board and carried into the tent. She couldn't move much of anything except her eyes. I was standing beside Brother Roberts when we laid hands on her and prayed.

She responded instantly. "Get these ropes off me!" she demanded.

Someone untied her, and the moment they did she jumped off that board and began running.

"I told you I'd get healed!" she shouted. "I told you I'd get healed!"

That girl had been expecting her miracle.

I decided in those days to take that kind of expectancy with me right out of Brother Roberts' meetings and into others I attended. I wanted things like that to happen everywhere I went. One day, I saw in the Word that praying in tongues brings edification. So I said, "I'm going to pray in tongues whether I feel like it or not— and I'm going to expect to be edified!" That day I had to drive all day to get home, so I prayed in tongues the whole way— all day long! My throat was dry. My body was tired. I had no physical evidence of being edified, but the Word cannot lie and it said I would be.

After I got home that evening, we went to a meeting held in someone's living room. My body was still tired, but my expectation was in high gear. I thought, *I'm going to expect a miracle here!*

Someone was speaking to the people gathered there. My tired body was sitting down in that living room, but my spirit was jumping, shouting and running in circles. I was expecting God to show up.

After he spoke, the speaker asked, "Does anyone need prayer?"

The lady in front of me held up her hand.

"Brother Copeland," he asked, "would you minister to her?"

"Yes!" I said, "Hallelujah!"

Then I attacked her with every ounce of faith I had. I didn't know if it was doing her any good or not, but I was blessed. I jumped up, started preaching, praying and laying hands on her. People started yelling, "Yes, amen!"

Sure enough, God moved. Not because I was anything special—but because He's something special and His Word is true. He wants to move. He wants to set people free. He wants to work miracles. So why shouldn't we expect them?

Kenneth

In the early years Kenneth did it all—he preached and ministered to the sick. Later, God called Gloria to teach on healing—and lay hands on everyone who needed healing.

On May 4, 1986—nearly 20 years and much fruit since they first arrived at Oral Roberts University—Kenneth received an honorary Doctor of Divinity for "teaching others how to replace failure and defeat with victory through the power of the Word of God." Gloria received an honorary Doctor of Humane Letters for "teaching God's people how to live victoriously in this life and for her commitment to a healing and deliverance ministry."

CHAPTER 4

The Call to the Nations

Ye have not chosen me, but I have chosen you, and ordained you, that ye should go and bring forth fruit, and that your fruit should remain.... JOHN 15:16

arch of 1967 was a turning point in my life. I was learning so much at ORU traveling with Brother Roberts, going to classes during the day and listening to Brother Hagin's tapes at night. I was watching Brother Roberts do by faith what I was hearing Brother Hagin teach.

I came home from school one afternoon so agitated in my spirit that I knew I had to be alone with God. I had known all day that He was trying to say something to me. Our house was only a block from the Arkansas River bed, so I went down there to pray and to listen.

I don't know what I was expecting, but it wasn't what I heard. I hadn't known God long enough back then to understand that He always thinks *big*.

He told me exactly what He was calling me to do. He was calling me to preach the gospel to the nations. In fact, He said in the last days, nations would be won in a day (some of them even by this ministry).

There I was as poor as a field mouse, driving an old Oldsmobile in need of a miracle, living in a little rent house—and I was called to the nations. He spoke to me for about two hours that afternoon. He commissioned me into this ministry.

He said things that I had no idea how I would ever be able to do, but I said yes to it all. I began meditating on what He said.

I studied it and fasted over it, off and on, until summer came. By that time, faith had come. Fear had gone. And one day about the first of June, I stood up before the Lord and said, "I'll tell You what I'm going to do. I'm going to preach the gospel of Jesus Christ. I'm going to preach that He saves, He heals, He baptizes with His Spirit and that He's coming again. I'm going to preach that Your Word is powerful and true. I'm going to preach it from the top of the world to the bottom, and I'm going to preach it all the way around the middle, and I am not going to compromise."

Somebody asked me how I planned on doing that.

By faith in God's Word!

Kenneth

Years ago down in that Tulsa riverbed, God told Ken that He had called us to a worldwide ministry. He commissioned us to the *nations!*

I thought, *Are you kidding? Nations? We hardly have enough money to drive to Fort Worth!* It was clear to me that God hadn't checked the balance in our checking account.

How are we going to minister to nations? I wondered.

Would you like to know what I discovered?

When God calls you to something, you start where you are.

We started out believing God to put food on our table.

You may laugh, but that was a stretch of faith for us back then.

Today, we're still stretching our faith, believing God—not for the money to feed our own family, but for the money to feed His! It takes millions and millions of dollars to get the meat of God's Word to the nations of the world. And you know what? God *still* doesn't check the balance in our bank account before He asks us to do something. It doesn't bother us though. We've learned that's just the way He is.

Gloria

The first day I was on my own in the ministry, I woke up and said, "Bless God, here I go!" I got out of bed, put on the only suit I owned, picked up my Bible and a yellow pad, and went to my office. It didn't take long to get there.

I walked from the bedroom to the living room.

I couldn't have gone much farther, because I didn't have enough money to get out of sight. I sat down to study my Bible and said, "Lord, I'm on call."

God started revealing some things to me which, in retrospect, were critical to the future of this ministry. I knew He wanted Gloria and me to agree and settle certain things forever. Number one, that we will never ask a man for a place to preach. Number two, that we will never ask people for money to get us by. Number three, that we will never ever preach anywhere at any time based on a financial arrangement.

Gloria and I sat down at the kitchen table and agreed with God about those three things. We'd no sooner done it than the devil spoke up, *You're whipped before you ever got out the front door! How in the world will anyone ask you to preach? No one knows where you are! Besides, how will you ever have anything financially? Why...*

"Satan, shut up!" I demanded. "That's God's problem, not mine!"

The phone rang while we were still sitting there. It was Harold Nichols, pastor of Grace Temple Church in Fort Worth, Texas.

"Brother Kenneth," he asked, "could you come have a meeting for me?"

I wanted to say, "Just a minute, I'll have to check my schedule." The only problem was that I didn't *have* a schedule.

"I'll be there," I said.

I've been going ever since.

Kenneth

FAITH SEMINAR

Conducted by:

KENNETH COPELAND

Beginning March 19th through March 30

These will be teaching sessions on how to exercise YOUR faith and get 100% results.

CALVARY TEMPLE

9th and Philadelphia   Pastor, Roy H. Sprague

hen I decided to live by faith, I discovered that my faith was well-developed on the negative side, but it seemed almost nonexistent on the positive side. I noticed that whenever I spoke something positive by faith, it was a real struggle to see it come to pass. Yet, when I'd say something negative, it would come to pass fast and easy.

"Why is that?" I asked the Lord.

Out of the abundance of the heart, He said.

My lightning-fast mind grasped the fact that I was getting just exactly what I was putting in my heart in abundance. If 10 percent of what I put in my heart was the Word, then 10 percent is what I would get. If I put 20 percent in, I'd get 20 percent out. If I put 50 percent in, I'd get 50 percent out. Therefore, if 100 percent of what I put in my heart was the Word of God, then 100 percent of what would come

out would be the Word!

In my case, I'd been putting 1 percent of the Word in my heart, and 99 percent junk.

So every time I got my back against a wall, junk came out my mouth!

When I worked in insurance with my dad, I heard a sales instructor say, "Samson killed 10,000 Philistines with the jawbone of an ass. There have been 10 times that many sales killed with the same weapon." That's the way I must have sounded to God. Christians use their mouths to destroy their healing, their prosperity and a lot of other blessings from God.

I realized that the best thing I could do was surround myself with the Word of God. If I wanted 100 percent results, I'd have to fill my heart with the Word 100 percent.

I started looking for ways Satan had been feeding me. The first thing I noticed

In 1968, Kenneth was ordained by Hilton Sutton at Faith Memorial Church in Houston, Texas.

was that there was a radio everywhere I looked. I turned them off. I turned off the radio in my car. I turned off the television. I stopped reading the newspaper.

"I'm going to fast these things for two weeks," I told the Lord.

That was in 1967, and I'm still fasting most of those things. I just never had time to get back to them. Instead, I started replacing the devil's junk food with God's stuff.

I got a reel-to-reel tape player that ran off four flashlight batteries. I could get an hour out of four batteries, but the last 10 minutes the tape moved mighty slow.

What I needed next was every tape by Brother Hagin that I could get my hands on. I drove my old car over to Brother Hagin's headquarters. His son-in-law, Buddy Harrison, was his general manager. I'd never met him, but I introduced myself and told him I'd been called to preach.

"I need Brother Hagin's tapes," I explained. "Here is the title to my car. I'll send you every offering I get until I pay for them."

"No, that's all right," Buddy said. "I don't need the title to your car. Here are the tapes."

Years later he said, "I *saw* that car! I thought, *My goodness, I don't want the title to that car! We teach prosperity. What if somebody sees that thing parked in front of our office?*"

Buddy told me later that he would have given me the tapes just to get me to get my car out of his parking lot. From that day on, old or not, that car became a classroom of faith and power.

I knew my heart needed to be filled to overflowing with the Word, so I locked myself in the garage. "Gloria," I said, "don't call me more than once for a meal. If I don't show up in five minutes, eat without me. I'll come in at night and sleep, but all the rest of the time I'll be in the garage. I don't want the kids coming through the door. I don't want *anybody* out there. If someone calls, just tell them I'm unavailable."

I took my Bible and my tape recorder to the garage and made myself available to God.

I stayed out there seven days. The first day, I listened to tapes for 13 hours. The second day, I was out there for close to 15 hours. From then on I averaged 18 hours a day.

After listening to those tapes night and day for nearly two weeks, I drove to Lubbock, Texas, where I'd been invited to preach for the Full Gospel Business-men at Furr's Cafeteria. I must have preached about 14 of Brother Hagin's tapes in about 45 minutes!

The Word says that *"out of the abundance of the heart the mouth speaks"* (Matthew 12:34, *New King James Version).* I was a living testimony that the verse was true. I preached all the way around that room, then went to the kitchen and preached to all the help.

The Methodists, Presbyterians and Baptists were saying, "Wow, Revival!" The Pentecostals were shouting, "Wildfire!"

People got healed, changed and delivered in that meeting.

There was such an *abundance* of the Word in my heart, that there was enough to meet my needs, to get that old car to Lubbock and back, and plenty left over to meet the needs of others.

I discovered that trying to let the light of the Lord shine through my life without the Word of God overflowing in my heart, was like trying to live off the power of four little flashlight batteries.

They'll work fine for a time. But after a while, they'll run as dry as I was before I locked myself in the garage with God and His Word.

You might say I plugged into the *Power.*

The day God commissioned me to this ministry in 1967, He said, *Your wife is precious to Me. I have given her to you. She will be to you what temper is to steel.*

If you know anything about steel, it's worthless until it's tempered, because it's brittle. Make a knife from steel that hasn't been tempered and it'll break. But when it's tempered, it becomes flexible enough to bend without breaking. Then and only then, will it keep an edge and be useful as a tool.

As I look back over 30 years in the ministry, I know that just like steel that hadn't been tempered, I could have broken if God hadn't given Gloria the grace to temper my life. Next to the Lord Jesus Himself, Gloria is the greatest gift God has ever given me.

K e n n e t h

As soon as Gloria and I agreed to God's rules regarding this ministry, Brother Nichols called and invited me to preach. He wanted me to come for four days, but God moved so mightily that I stayed for three weeks. It was a glorious time, but when the meeting was over, I didn't have anything booked.

"Where are you going from here?" Brother Nichols asked.

"To the car," I said. Brother Nichols knew that I was being careful in how I responded, so he went along with me.

"Well, I'll go with you." We went to my car and sat in the front seat. After a minute, Brother Nichols started praying. "Lord," he said, "this man of God helped my church, and I want to help see to it that his ministry goes right on down the road. I know that wherever he goes, congregations like mine will be helped. I'm setting myself in agreement with him for a full schedule."

God answered that prayer. We didn't have one bit of slack. Hilton Sutton called from Houston and asked me to come for a few days. I stayed three weeks. When that meeting ended, Hilton's dad, who pastored a church in Beaumont, Texas, was there.

"Brother Kenneth," he said, "Hilton called me and told me how you were preaching. I want to tell you something. This is the kind of preaching I heard a number of years ago. The Assemblies of God grew out of this kind of preaching. You set my spirit on fire. Can you come preach in my church?"

I agreed to go, and later when I arrived the first thing he said was, "I have to tell you something. I couldn't guarantee you $50 if you stayed a month."

"Sir," I said, "if you guaranteed me $50, I wouldn't have come."

"Bless God! That's what I wanted to hear you say."

"What's happened to your church?" I asked.

"We've got a flu epidemic," he said. "I don't have more than three people in the whole congregation who aren't sick."

The first night, we had six people at the meeting. Brother Sutton brought me the offering in a paper sack. He knew there wasn't much in it, so he didn't even count it. He stuffed the bag in my pocket.

Later that night, I counted it.
$4.25.

The next morning two people showed up—counting Brother Sutton's wife. After the service, I went to my room and shut the door. Mrs. Sutton knocked on the door and said, "Supper's ready, Brother Copeland."

"You all go ahead and eat."

I just stayed before God. "Lord," I said, "what in the world am I going to do?" I started worrying. *Maybe I should run an ad in the paper.*

Then I realized that if I ran a full-page ad in the paper it wouldn't do any good, because nobody knew who I was. I paced that room saying, "Lord, what am I going to do? What am I going to do? What am I going to do?"

It was 2 o'clock in the morning when I had a stunning revelation.

This isn't doing any good.

I quit pacing and fell to my knees. "Lord," I asked, "in the Name of Jesus, what's happening here?"

I sent you there, didn't I? He asked. "Yes, Sir."

Didn't I tell you I'd take care of you? "Yes…"

Didn't I take care of you at Oral Roberts University?

"Yes, Sir."

Why do you think I won't take care of you here?

I thought He wasn't taking care of me, because the circumstances looked that way. In other words, I was walking by sight, not by faith.

During all the hours I'd spent worrying, I kept hearing *1 Peter 5:6-7* on the inside of me. I hadn't paid too much attention to it, because it didn't sound like God's voice. It sounded like Brother Hagin.

Kenneth preaches what the Lord has given him whether two or 10,000 are in attendance.

I flipped over to 1 Peter 5:6-7. *Humble yourself under the mighty hand of the Lord, casting all your care over on Him, for He cares for you. Be sober and be vigilant. Resist the devil* (see verses 6-9).

"Father," I prayed, "I'm determined to get out of the flesh. I'm determined to stop being moved by what I see." I started praying in the Spirit. After a while, I began to see some things in my heart. I decided to do the same thing I'd heard Brother Hagin say he had done in the same situation.

"Lord," I said, "this meeting is my care, because I care about it. I care about these people. I care about Brother Sutton. I care about these people learning to walk by faith. I care about them being healed from the flu. I care about revival in this church. You've sent me here to do a job that I care about.

"But now, based on 1 Peter 5:6-7, I roll all my care over onto You. I'm not going to touch it with my thought life."

Afterward, every time I'd think about it, I'd say, "No, Satan, I refuse that thought. I don't have a care. This meeting isn't my concern. I don't care if anyone comes or not."

I told the Lord, "I don't care if anyone except those two women show up. I don't care if there are only six. I'm going to preach what You tell me to preach. I'm going to preach like there are 10,000 people there. I'll never change a message because no one showed up. I'll preach the same sermon to empty seats. You'll have to take care of the money. You'll have to take care of the people. You'll have to get them saved and filled with the Holy Spirit.

"I'm going to *preach!*" I got up and started running around that little bedroom. "Bless God, I don't have a care!"

I went into that little church and preached! I preached up one aisle and down another. I preached to four, six and eight people.

"Do you have a bottle of oil?" I asked Brother Sutton.

"Yes, I do," he said, grinning.

"Then let's go get these people healed."

One by one, we anointed those folks with oil, laid hands on them and prayed. They came staggering out of bed by faith—sweating, coughing and blowing. But when they planted their feet on the floor, they were healed. Everyone got healed except one deacon who refused to get out of bed. He stayed sick for over two more weeks because he wouldn't act on God's Word.

News of what happened reached the beauty shop. From there it spread faster than the flu.

I learned then that if you can't get the people to God, take God to the people. He'll be happy to heal them anywhere.

Kenneth

One of the reasons I let the circumstances of that Beaumont meeting nudge me out of faith was because I missed Gloria's birthday while I was there. I didn't have any idea how I was going to get her a birthday present. The $4.25 offering I received wouldn't have paid for my gas home, much less anything for her birthday.

The Lord had told me that the Beaumont meeting would be the turning point of my ministry. There were times when I wondered which way He was turning it. I was preaching to an almost empty church house, while Gloria was at home believing that God was the Lord of our finances.

I got into agreement with her, and not only confessed that Jesus was the Lord of our finances, I confessed over and over that Jesus was the Lord over the finances of that meeting. Brother Sutton was still stuffing the offering sacks into my pocket each night after the service. Finally, I took one of those paper sacks and poured all the change into it. I told the Lord, "I'm taking this sack full of change home to Gloria for her birthday. Jesus, You're Lord over this."

By the time that meeting was over, we'd had one of the best meetings of my life. Since I was confessing that Jesus was Lord over the finances, it was also one of the best meetings financially that I've ever had. We had an absolute runaway.

I was so thrilled when I got home. I handed Gloria that sack of change and said, "Happy birthday!" I hadn't counted it, so I had no idea how much was in it.

We got in the car and headed down to a place where she'd seen some shoes and a purse she wanted. We were so happy! We had the time of our lives that day buying that purse and pair of shoes.

When Gloria got ready to pay, she handed the sack of change to the sales clerk. The clerk couldn't believe what she was seeing. She opened the sack and poured it out on the counter. Then they flattened out all the coins and she started counting. When she finished, there was about 35 cents left over. The sales clerk handed Gloria that little dab of change and said, "Well, one thing is for sure, I broke you!"

Gloria had been training her tongue to be hair-trigger fast on positive confessions.

"No you didn't!" she said. "There's more where that came from!"

Of course, we didn't have any more right then. But we had made Jesus the Lord of our finances.

And *God* is never broke!

Kenneth

The lesson the Lord taught me in Beaumont, Texas, has been responsible for 99 percent of the success Gloria and I have had in the ministry. Why? Because circumstances have presented us never-ending opportunities to cast our cares upon the Lord.

Sometime after the meeting in Beaumont, I went to California. We rented a little church facility out there from what we thought was an interdenominational church. I discovered later that it wasn't.

When the people who owned the building found out what I was preaching, they weren't one bit happy. They wanted to throw me out, but I'd signed a contract with them. So, they decided on another way to get rid of me.

They moved me to a different building every night, in hopes no one would find my meeting. It's a good thing I was walking by faith, and staying in love. Otherwise, I might have really acted ugly.

On one particular night, they set up my podium and my little sound system in what looked like a living room. I almost never found it. If *I* couldn't find my meeting, I figured the handful of people who'd been coming wouldn't find it either.

In spite of the move, 17 people showed up that night. I opened my Bible to my text and said, "Lord, I roll all the care of this over onto You. I've come to preach."

While I was preaching, the door beside me opened. It led into a kitchen where all the food was being prepared for a banquet in another building. A guy came out of the kitchen carrying a big tray of food. He walked right in front of me, between the front row of people and me and out another door!

A little while later, another guy walked in front of me carrying two buckets. Both men looked surprised to see me. I never paused or stopped preaching. Then another one came. Pretty soon, there was a steady stream of people walking

in front of me.

But I had cast the care of the meeting over onto God.

I preached solid for an hour and a half. I never stopped. I gave it everything I had. In fact, I had *fun!* I could have reached out and grabbed any of those men. Once, I walked alongside one of them, all the way to the door. He said, "Amen!"

"Yeah, *amen!*" I agreed.

There were only 17 people there to begin with, and all of them were already saved and filled with the Holy Ghost. When the service was over, the devil started pressuring me. *Boy, you ripped it tonight. That was a terrible service, and you wasted your time. There probably isn't 89 cents in that offering.*

I was smiling real big. "It doesn't make any difference to me," I told Satan under my breath. "I'm not bound to an offering. Money comes to me from everywhere."

About then, a man walked up to me. "That beat all I've ever seen," he said. "I've never seen anybody preach with a solid stream of cooks and waiters walking in front of them."

"Well," I said, "I rolled the care of it over onto the Lord."

"Copeland," he said, "I'm not saying this for the fun of it. I'm telling you this from the Holy Ghost. If you keep that up,

Kenneth has preached in some unusual places.

you'll fill every major convention hall in this nation, because the devil can't daunt you. He can't scare you. He can't back you off."

That man not only encouraged me in the Lord, he helped me get the right equipment to duplicate our meeting tapes. He became a good friend and helped my ministry immeasurably in many ways. What the devil tried to do for harm, God turned for good.

I've been in some places where I would never have made it out alive if it hadn't been for the power of God. I was ministering in the middle of a parking lot at the fairgrounds of a West Texas town one time, when I looked up and saw the meanest-looking man I'd ever seen— coming straight at me!

Before I was saved I ran up against some pretty mean dudes, but none of them compared to this fellow. He had a scar that started just above his right eye and ran all the way down his cheek, under his chin and into his collar.

"Jesus, here he comes!" I said, as he started toward me with his teeth gritted.

I just kept on preaching. "Greater is He that is in me than he that is in the world."

He came closer.

And closer.

Finally, he reached me…

God melted him in his tracks.

"Pray for me!" he begged.

I prayed for him and led him to the Lord.

A year later, I was preaching at a Full Gospel Businessmen's meeting, when a fellow walked up front to meet me. He had a big grin on his face. "Brother Copeland…Brother Copeland…Brother Copeland!" he said, sticking out his hand. "You don't remember me, do you?"

"No." I knew there was something familiar about him, but I didn't recall ever having met this man.

"I'm the one you laid hands on out there in a parking lot in Lubbock, Texas."

I looked a little closer. A year earlier, that scar was the most outstanding thing about that man. This time I didn't even notice it. The Word of God had completely changed his countenance. Eternal life had even made him *look* like a new creature.

"I just wanted you to know," he said, "I'm preaching the gospel."

The Bible says that you can still see the scars Jesus bore from the cross.

Because of the Cross, you can hardly see this man's scars.

You simply see *Jesus*.

Kenneth

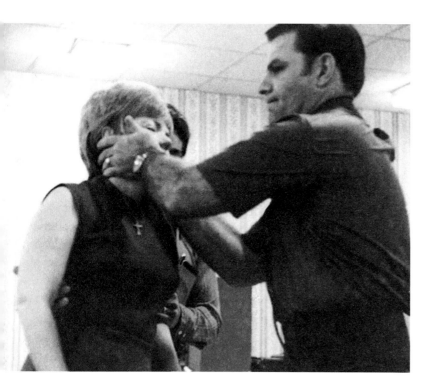

"Lord," I said, "if You want me to preach there, You'll have to set it up, because I'm not a good enough judge. If You left it up to me, I'd be in the wrong place at the wrong time. You called me, so I believe You can handle it."

I showed up at that meeting and took a chair. Nobody knew me from Hogan's goat. The man who was the head of that chapter walked by and looked at me. A little later, he walked by again. I could tell the Lord was bugging him. I acted like I didn't see him.

Finally, he walked up to me and said, "Who are you, Brother?"

"My name is Copeland."

"Great, it's good to have you."

"Thank you, it's good to be here."

He was really bothered, but he went ahead and started the meeting. I just sat there and didn't say a thing. *Now you've missed God,* the devil assured me.

"No, I didn't miss God. God said He wanted me here, and I'm here. That's as far as I go. I can't heal anyone. I can't save anyone. I'm just God's boy. He's the boss. I'm where I was told to be."

After a while, the man came back over to me. "What business are you in?"

"I'm with the Lord."

"Are you a preacher?"

"Yes."

"Well, it's good to have you with us."

"It's good to be here."

About halfway through the service, he said, "Brother back there," pointing to

There were times when the Lord told me I was supposed to preach somewhere, but I wasn't asked. When that happened, I just showed up and kept my mouth shut. First, the Lord told me to never ask a man for a place to preach. Second, I knew if I got involved, I'd foul it up.

Once, the Lord told me He wanted me to speak at a particular Full Gospel Businessmen's meeting. I didn't know a soul in that chapter, and it wouldn't have mattered if I did.

me, "it seems to me that you have something from the Lord."

"Yes, amen," I said, walking to the podium.

God has proven time and time again, that when He gives me a message, I won't have to push the door open to find a place to deliver it.

I just trust Him.

He will make a way. And His way always works.

Kenneth

ƒor years I tried to decide to lose weight. I knew my health was in jeopardy. At one time, I weighed 80 pounds more than I do today. When I *finally* decided to do something about it, the Lord said, *You don't have a weight problem.*

"I don't?"

No, you don't have a weight problem.

"I thought I did."

No, that's not your problem.

"What is the problem then, Lord?"

You're a hypocrite.

"Ouch! Lord, that hurt!"

Yes, but you're still a hypocrite.

"Lord, if You say I'm a hypocrite, I must be. How am I being hypocritical?"

You would never let anyone put the wrong brand of oil, much less the wrong weight of oil, in your vehicles.

"Yes, Sir," I admitted, "I'd scream like a mashed cat if someone didn't do the right kind of maintenance on my car, tractor or my airplane."

Yet, you stick stuff in your mouth then into your body all the time. You have no idea what it is. You don't bother to read the label. If it smells good and tastes good, you eat it. I said in My Word to beware of the king's meat, because it's deceitful.

"What does deceitful mean?"

*It looks good. It tastes good. But it's **not** good.* I swallowed hard. This was hitting home.

I said in My Word that a man given to appetite should put a knife to his throat.

"What's a knife?"

*The sword of the Word of God. The right reason to put the sword to your throat is because of your health, not just because of your weight. If you change what you **eat,** your weight will take care of itself.*

You have to understand that when I was a young boy, many times I'd come home after school and eat a whole pie by myself. After I was grown, I'd go to a bakery and buy a whole loaf of fresh bread. I'd punch a hole in the end of the loaf and push a stick of butter inside. Then I'd eat it.

I *really* didn't like vegetables.

Now the Lord told me in no uncertain terms to get my attention *off* my weight and *on* my eating habits. I realized that the change would have to come from the inside out. I put the sword of the Word of God to my throat and put a stop to deceitful meat. Over time, I lost those excess pounds. In the process, I developed a desire for broccoli, cauliflower, carrots and all kinds of good, healthy things to eat.

After the Lord called me into the ministry, I lost 80 pounds. I only owned one suit, and I kept taking it to a Spanish man who altered it for me. I took my britches down there one time and he said, "Hey, Brother Copeland, I want to tell you something."

"What?"

"If you fix those pants once more, you're going to have one big pocket in the back!" He laughed so hard, I thought he was going to fall over.

"Take them up again," I said with a smile.

The Word of God had literally made me a new man.

Kenneth

Sometimes people attend one of our meetings today, see throngs of people and think that's the way it's always been. I have news for you—it *hasn't* always been that way.

It was the biggest part of 10 years before we were consistently having 300 or more people. For years and years people stayed away from our meetings in *crowds.*

We rented an old, dirty drugstore for our first meeting outside of a church. Ken preached to a few hundred people and duplicated his own tapes.

We rented a building at the fairgrounds in Lubbock one time. We'd hired a couple of people by then, and we had to pay them. I was the photographer. I was the accountant. I carried the offering—what little there was—around in my purse.

We rented a building, and about 25 people showed up.

What did Ken do?

Preached the Word of God.

We kept on doing exactly what God told us to do.

We were still living in Tulsa, and between Ken's meetings we didn't sit home and rest. That first year in ministry, we went to every one of Brother Hagin's services. During one of those seminars, an ice storm covered the streets for several days, but we did not miss a service. We slipped and slid our way over there and back, praying in tongues every day and every night. In bad weather, there wouldn't be more than a handful of people there. In good weather, there were about 250.

In between Brother Hagin's meetings, we listened to tapes.

We totally immersed ourselves in the Word of God.

There were a lot of people who attended nearly every one of Brother Hagin's meetings, but not all of those people took the Word and did what we did. Some heard the Word and got blessed but did not change their way of life.

Many heard the Word, but they didn't *do* it.

We didn't just go listen and not pay attention to it. We heard the Word with a heart to *do* it.

That's what you have to do.

I never walked in victory until I began to feed on the Word with full intention to obey it. I immersed myself in it until my soul—my mind, will and emotions—became subject to what God said instead of what the world says.

A lot of people would have been discouraged by preaching to one small group of people after another. We were no different. Many times we got discouraged, too. But we did not quit. It is not always easy to obey God, but it is always rewarding if you just continue doing what you are told to do.

Thank God we had renewed our minds to be subject to the Word instead of circumstances. Otherwise we would have fallen in the same trap.

The truth is that God so loved the world, those small crowds didn't bother Him.

Jesus would have died for *one.*

G l o r i a

One day about 30 years ago, I was reading the Word and praying in the back bedroom of our little house in Tulsa, Oklahoma. As I read my Bible, one verse just exploded with meaning in my heart. It said that no man says "Jesus is Lord" except by the Holy Ghost.

If you could only say it by the Holy Ghost, I decided I was going to say it *all the time!* I walked all over our little bedroom and said it all afternoon. "Jesus is Lord!

"Jesus is Lord over my body. Jesus is Lord over my mind. Jesus is Lord over my spirit. Jesus is Lord over this bedroom. Jesus is Lord over my clothes. Jesus is Lord over my car. Jesus is Lord over this ministry. Jesus is Lord over anything that has to do with me, because I make Jesus the Lord over my life."

When I was a kid in school, I thought about airplanes so much I drew them all over my book covers. I drew airplanes on my assignment sheets and my papers.

Here I was 30 years old, and I started scribbling "Jesus is Lord" on everything. I started signing my letters, "Jesus is Lord!" I had a plaque made and nailed it to the front door. It announced to every person who stepped onto our porch, "Jesus is Lord!"

On the first letter I ever wrote involving this ministry—it was called Kenneth Copeland Evangelistic Association back then—I wrote "Jesus is Lord" across the top of one page.

I have clothes with "Jesus is Lord" embroidered on them. Why? Because I became consumed with that truth. I don't say it to be cute, or just to end my broadcast, or to put on my stationery.

I'm consumed by the fact that Jesus *is* Lord.

The Bible says that every knee will bow, and every tongue confess that He is Lord, to the glory of God the Father. That means that someday *everyone,* Christian or not, will bow their knee and confess that He is Lord.

Why wait?

He is the undisputed Savior of the universe.

Every day, in every way, I want to say it to Him.

"Jesus, *You* are *my* Lord!"

Kenneth

As the ministry has grown and the logo has changed over the years, the message has remained the same... JESUS IS LORD!

Every Available Voice

And this gospel of the kingdom shall be preached in all the world

for a witness unto all nations… MATTHEW 24:14

When God called me into this ministry down in that Arkansas River bed, I saw the Word of God going forth to thousands of people. I clung to that vision in spite of the fact that after even five years in ministry, I hadn't yet preached to a crowd of 300.

While I was faithful to those first small steps, it seemed like to me I was just holding on the ramp. If I couldn't fly, at the very least I wanted to taxi to the runway.

Then in 1975, the Lord commanded me to *"preach the uncompromised Word of God on every available voice."* I felt like I finally had clearance to take off! Through voices like radio and television, I could reach the thousands that I'd seen in my spirit five years earlier in that riverbed experience.

But even in my excitement, I was aware of the tremendous demand such broadcasts would make on this ministry. I looked around at our resources and wondered how we could manage such an enormous task.

Then I remembered.

It's a journey of faith.

Kenneth

(Facing page)
Kenneth taping a
radio program.

I was astounded after the first meeting I had that we sold tapes of the services. People ordered *98 tapes!* I never even *imagined* selling that many tapes. For several days I was up until almost 4 in the morning making copies—one reel at a time.

Then one day, someone mentioned a man's name and said he had sold 20,000 tapes in one year. *They must have that number wrong,* I thought.

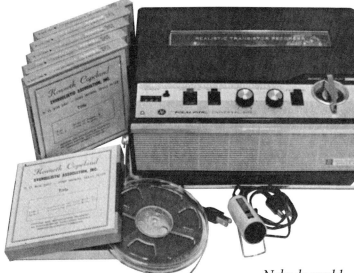

Nobody could sell 20,000 tapes in a year. Of course, they *had* sold that many tapes, but until then I didn't know it was possible. Why? Because until then, I hadn't realized how God could multiply my time and His Word by spreading the gospel through tapes. That 20,000 figure helped me set a faith goal, and I began to pray. I realized, though,

that if I was going to believe God to sell 20,000 tapes, I'd have to give and sow a *lot* of tapes as seed.

So I began planting tapes. I just started giving them to preachers and ministries by the handfuls. That was no small sacrifice, since I was the one sitting up all night making copies. Afterward, when the Lord provided us with a duplicator, I almost kissed it every time I walked by.

Back in those days, I did a lot of preaching for other people. I preached for Full Gospel Businessmen's Fellowship, churches and other ministries. Before the service, people would say, "Now, Brother Copeland, we want you to be sure and mention your tapes from the pulpit."

"No," I'd say, "I can't do that."

I've never said that it was wrong for anyone else to do it, but I'd already told God *I* wouldn't. I couldn't go back on my word. The guy who did the recording for Full Gospel Businessmen's Fellowship used to get so frustrated with me. "Now, Kenneth," he'd say, "I want you to talk about your tapes."

"No."

"How are we ever going to sell them?"

"Let's *agree* that we'll sell them."

"Oh, that's all you ever say."

Later, he'd come back shaking his head. "It beats anything I've ever seen. You don't ever do anything! You never even mention that you have tapes. In fact, you just make it as hard on everybody as you can. Yet, by the end of the meeting, we sell more of your tapes than anyone's! I don't understand."

"I know you don't," I told him.

He didn't understand because he was never in any of the services. He was always out there making tapes. He wasn't hearing the Word.

I thank God for putting a stop to my small thinking and for His helping me move over into faith where tapes are concerned, because those tapes have gone literally all over the world. Some years ago, for example, I heard from a pastor who lived in the African country of Mozambique. His country was in the middle of a famine, and he was literally watching helplessly as his people died of starvation. Somehow, he got a set of tapes I'd taught on prosperity. On those tapes, I taught that God's Word works whether you have a dime or not. God doesn't base the gospel on what government is in power.

That man took hold of the Word of God and turned the tables on the devil. He attacked that famine with the Word. Pretty soon, his church was providing food for 1,000 starving people. Then, 2,000…3,000…4,000…5,000.

Before long, that church was providing food for *9,000 people!*

Did they sit back and relax when they reached the 9,000?

No! They set a new faith goal to feed 15,000 starving people.

God told me back in that riverbed that He was calling this ministry to the nations. In most cases, my tapes got there first.

Kenneth

Early on, God showed Kenneth how he could get the Word out—how God could multiply the time and the Word—by spreading the gospel through tapes.

I made some of my biggest mistakes, and learned some of my best lessons, through radio. I was preaching one time, flowing in the anointing of God's revelation, when I heard the Lord say, *Get on the radio.*

I didn't think twice. I just jumped out and got on a radio station. It turned out to be one of the most frustrating experiences of my life. First, I couldn't pay the bill. That bill just seemed to stagger me. (It was only about $35 a week!) If that weren't bad enough, I'd gotten on some kind of ignoramus station. I'd send them my tapes to broadcast, and they'd send them back with Communist propaganda on them!

It didn't matter how I tried, nothing about that deal would work—it never did. That experience drove me to my knees in prayer. This is what I learned: The Holy Spirit is always doing His job. He is always on duty. He is always leading. He is always speaking. I'd just been too dense to hear.

Thank God, the Lord sent Brother Hagin to explain some things to me. "The

Lord never changes," he said, "so watch His pattern in dealing with you. His patterns in dealing with you in the past reveal how He'll deal with you in the future."

I started looking at God's patterns in dealing with me, and I realized that He usually told me to do something a considerable amount of time before it was time to do it. I'm not talking about ministering to people. When I was at the pulpit and God told me to minister to someone, He expected me to get after it. But sometimes I'd be on the platform ministering under the anointing, when I'd see in the spirit that we were supposed to go on 50 more stations. When that happened, I'd stop and announce it right then. Afterward, I'd jump off the platform and go sign up on 50 stations.

Then I'd try to make it work.

I didn't realize that God was telling me that in advance, so I could get in the Word and build my faith for it. He was giving me time to prepare, but I didn't know it.

One time the Lord said, *You've mistaken the anointing for your own physical strength. You get under the anointing and see into your future, and commit to things you're not ready to do. When you get out from under the anointing, you don't have the physical strength left to accomplish it. You run ahead of My timing.*

Thank God for correcting me, because the pace was almost killing me.

There weren't enough days and nights to do all that I'd obligated myself to do.

The Holy Spirit was finally able to get through to me and let me know that I'd seen accurately that God wanted me to do many things, but not all at once! He'd planned on my doing them over a period of 10 years.

The reason it took so long to clear up that misunderstanding was that God had to deal with me on the run. I had become too busy in ministry to spend quiet time with Him. Without that quiet time in the Word and in God's presence, you can't let the Lord lead you correctly. Some things that just look wonderful aren't from God at all, but you'll never know it until you slow down and get quiet with Him.

After that first radio fiasco, the devil taunted me, *God isn't going to let you on television. You've flopped on one radio station.*

In part, that was the truth. I *had* flopped on that radio station.

But I got quiet with the Lord and found His timing. That year I had to believe God harder than I'd ever believed up until that time. We closed the year on 35 stations. The following year, we closed the year on 700 stations.

That year our broadcast became the fastest-growing religious broadcast in radio history. Leave it to God to take a flop and turn it into the victory of a lifetime!

Kenneth

e published our first *Believer's Voice of Victory* magazine in September of 1973. At that time, it was just a newsletter going to 3,000 people. By 1975, our circulation had grown to 20,000. When George Pearsons came on staff, he started our art department, then took over the magazine.

George's father had been a production manager for a major New York advertising art studio in the 1950s that produced ads for magazines such as *Time, Life* and *Look*. George had the same pioneering spirit. He and the editorial staff began adapting the style of our magazine to those like *Time*. His purpose wasn't to use magazines like *Time* as a goal. The goal was to go *beyond* anything the world could reach.

There's a ceiling on worldly publications that we don't have. They can't reach beyond where they are into the realm of the *anointing*. Yet, the whole purpose of our magazine is to present the Word of God on paper *through* the anointing.

George had read a little article by John G. Lake about how he used to pray over the letters he sent out. He believed

God to transmit the anointing on those papers. That's exactly what all of us here at the ministry were believing. Before an issue was mailed, the staff gathered to pray, releasing their faith that people would be healed when they reached into the mailbox to take out the magazine. Before long we began getting reports of that happening.

Over the years, *Believer's Voice of Victory* grew from a newsletter to a full-spread magazine. We added articles by people such as Jerry Savelle, Charles Capps, Mac Hammond, Lynne Hammond, Jesse Duplantis, Creflo Dollar and others.

People's lives were affected so dramatically by the teaching, that letters began pouring into the office. Those letters gave birth to the testimony articles that we run in each issue.

Today, *Believer's Voice of Victory* is mailed monthly to more than half a million homes in 135 different countries on five different continents!

It's exciting to know that the Good News is being spread throughout the world on the powerful voice of the printed page. But there is something that excites me even more...to see God at work through those pages.

Here's an example.

Wayne and Jo Ann Harrison's testimony was featured in the May 1991 issue of *Believer's Voice of Victory.* In that magazine, Jo Ann told how she had been digging into the Word of God for faith when her husband, Wayne, died at home of an apparent heart attack. Efforts to resuscitate him didn't help.

He was pronounced dead on arrival at the hospital.

Jo Ann knew her rights, and she wouldn't give up even in the face of an apparent staggering defeat.

In a stunning display of God's glory, the same power that raised Jesus from the dead raised Wayne Harrison. It was a wonderful testimony!

Months later, on another continent, John Forde and his wife, Jennie, were struggling to pastor their church in Lethem, Guyana. They were doing a great work for God there, ministering to two tribes of Indians, the Wapishianans and the Macus—most of whom had never heard the uncompromised Word of God. But the Fordes were under an attack of the devil.

Their newborn son, delivered months prematurely and weighing only 31.5 ounces, had just been pronounced dead in a Brazilian hospital. John was stunned by the news.

Nurses had disconnected all life support. The baby, they said, was gone.

Twenty-four hours earlier, John Forde might have given up hope in the face of such a report. But not now.

On his way to the hospital, he had read and re-read the May 1991 issue of *Believer's Voice of Victory*. A friend from England had mailed it to him.

He'd read the magazine once, but at the urging of the Holy Spirit, he'd read it again—cover to cover—on his way to the hospital. Once again he read Kenneth's teaching that faith is a servant. Once again he read about the woman whose husband had been raised from the dead.

John had heard the Word...and faith had come. Standing in the hospital, he stretched his hands toward his lifeless son. "Father," John prayed, "I claim the life of my child! The woman whose story was in *Believer's Voice of Victory* stood on Your Word. I stand on the same Word. You are no respecter of persons. If You did it for her, You'll do it for me.

"Now, I rebuke the spirit of death and command it to loose its hold on my son. Faith is my servant, and I release it to bring forth a miracle in the Name of Jesus!"

Sure enough, tiny John Everton Forde Jr. revived.

Spontaneously. Inexplicably.

Today, he is 6 years old, and in perfect health.

I am thrilled that *Believer's Voice of Victory* is mailed to half a million homes in 135 countries on five continents. But the changing lives excite me more than the changing numbers.

A woman in one part of the United States stands on God's Word for a miracle. The story is written and published in another part of the United States. It's mailed to England. At the leading of the Holy Spirit, someone in England mails it to Guyana. That man of God has it in his hand in *Brazil* the day his baby dies—and his baby is raised up.

Believers...*that's Victory!*

Gloria

1995 Believers' Convention

think only of God and His Word—a time to receive the ministry of the Holy Spirit.

So, in 1978, we held our first week-long convention in Anaheim, California. It was a powerful time in the Lord, and we continue to hold a meeting there each year. Later, we added the Southwest Believers' Convention in Fort Worth to our schedule of annual meetings. There have also been East Coast Believers' Conventions in Atlanta, Georgia, and Charlotte, North Carolina. In time, we added international conventions in England, Australia and South Africa.

Over the years, we have been blessed by a variety of speakers—great men and women of God like Hilton Sutton, Fred Price, T.L. Osborn, Norvel Hayes, Billye Brim, John Osteen, Happy Caldwell, Jerry Savelle, John Avanzini, Kenneth E. Hagin, Jesse Duplantis, R.W. Schambach, Creflo Dollar, Oral Roberts, Charles Capps and many others.

Now, instead of a station wagon, six 18-wheelers transport everything needed to conduct the Believers' Conventions. And instead of just Gloria, me and the kids, we take as many as 50 people on the road to help with everything that has to be done.

When Gloria and I first began holding meetings, we loaded up the station wagon, believed God and hit the road. Since very few people knew who we were, it took about two and a half weeks before we had a crowd. Back then, our meetings were usually three weeks long, and a crowd of 100 was common. Later, as the ministry grew, we had three-day meetings two or three times a month—usually 25 to 30 each year.

Eventually, we had our own band and backup singers who traveled and ministered with us. God manifested Himself mightily in those meetings, but we began to see that three-day meetings weren't enough. Somehow, people needed to be totally immersed in the Word of God for at least a week. They needed a time of being saturated with the Word—a time to

God has put together a group of people who work as a team. Early on, the Lord brought Jerry Savelle to minister alongside us. In 1978, Len Mink, a well-known television personality who'd walked away from his career to follow the Lord, joined the team as praise and worship leader. In time, the Lord added Jesse Duplantis. Then, Creflo Dollar.

I never tell anyone what to preach. On Sunday night before the convention, we get together and share what God has put on our hearts. Always, the Lord has one main theme, and He gives each one of us a part of it to preach.

Exciting is too mild a word to describe 10,000 people worshiping God and offering the sacrifice of praise. *Glorious* is more like it! I've seen waves of glory sweep over the crowd.

People come from all over the world to these conventions. Usually 25 to 40 countries and at least 48 states from the United States are represented—sometimes all 50!

There aren't enough books to document all the miracles God has performed in the meetings over the years. I'll never forget one little boy whose mother brought him to Healing School. He'd been born without any nostrils. They simply weren't there. Doctors were going to surgically

The current ministry team (left to right): Jerry Savelle, Len Mink, Jesse Duplantis and Creflo Dollar.

form nostrils, but the *Creator* did it instead. God performed a miracle right there in the healing line. The child developed nostrils—openings where there had been none!

Men have been healed of AIDS.

One man, who had been planning a murder, repented and gave his heart to the Lord.

Discouraged ministers have had their ministry resurrected.

God has caused those once-small meetings to become large conventions, but that isn't what really matters to me. I recently preached to 23 people in Cold Bay, Alaska. I can tell you from my own heart, and from God's heart, it's not about numbers—it's about love.

If you only remember one thing about Believers' Conventions, remember this:

ONE WORD FROM GOD CAN CHANGE YOUR LIFE FOREVER.

K e n n e t h

In 1979, Gloria held the first Healing School.

*I*n the summer of 1979, someone sent me a letter with a word from the Lord. *God has something He wants you to do.* We were up in the country at the time, and one morning I was on the porch praying. I thought of that prophecy and said, "Lord, if You have something You want me to do, You know I'll do it. Just let me know what it is."

I got up from prayer and went in to wash my hair. While I was washing it, the Lord spoke to me and said, *I want you to start teaching on healing in every meeting.*

Well, it shocked me. We'd lived healed for many years, and knew how to do it. Still, it had never occurred to me to teach someone else *how* to do it. I had never thought of my doing such a thing, and never would have. I did not want to have a speaking ministry. I was not comfortable on the platform. I had no aspirations to be there! I had always helped and supported Kenneth in the background and really that's where I wanted to stay. Furthermore, I wouldn't have picked *me* to do it. But it was the most powerful thing the Lord has ever spoken to me. I knew it was God! When Ken got up that morning, I told him. Ken has always, without reservation, supported me in following God. He didn't hesitate to do it again.

In September of 1979, we held our first Healing School in Atlanta.

The Lord said, *I want you to share what you know about being healed, because I want My people well.*

So I began to do that. Then, after a while, He said, *I want you to start laying hands on people.*

I didn't want to do that either. But He told me to, so I started doing it.

I'll tell you, it's been such a blessing to me to see people get healed and delivered. But God hasn't had me teach Healing Schools all these years so that I can get blessed.

He wants His people well.

I don't think most of us have any idea how passionate He is on the subject of your healing. He bought your healing with His own body. He is moved by the feeling of your infirmities.

The woman with an issue of blood just reached out in faith and touched His garment. In the Bible, you'll find Jesus always ready to heal. He is the same yesterday, today and forever.

Jesus has already done His part.

At Healing School, we just reach out by faith and do ours.

G l o r i a

One of the most powerful truths I've ever seen in the Bible since I became a Christian is the significance of our blood covenant with God. It's staggering to realize that the God of the universe approached a man named Abraham and cut a covenant with him. A covenant is a bond of everlasting friendship that goes beyond just knowing or trusting someone. It goes beyond the natural ties of being born to the same parents.

It's a covenant to live or to die for.

The Bible says that there is a friend who sticks closer than a brother.

It's the brotherhood of blood—Jesus' blood.

It's the most sacred of all unions.

That's why I preached about the blood covenant on August 28, 1982.

I didn't preach it to *a* church.

I preached it to what was probably the largest single gathering of *the Church* since Pentecost. It was a worldwide Communion service broadcast by satellite from the Southwest Believers' Convention to 200 locations in the United States and 20 cities around the world.

Think about it, only in this generation has the technology been available to link that many believers together. George Metcalf, a consultant from NASA, as quoted in the *Believer's Voice of Victory* magazine, August 1982, said, "This is the beginning of a new phase of Christians utilizing technology provided by God through the Space Program. Ten years ago (1972) this event would have been impossible. Today, satellites are in place both domestically and internationally to transmit a television signal that will cover the earth.

"The International Indian Ocean, Atlantic, and Pacific satellites, as well as the Western Union and RCA satellite systems will allow the World Communion Service to literally surround the globe. The magnitude of this project will require over 600 highly trained people throughout the world."

A direct satellite feed from Seoul, South Korea, allowed every participant to view Dr. Paul Yonggi Cho, pastor of the

largest church in the world, partake of the Communion with us. By a "split screen" picture, they could see us and we could see them. This is all pretty common now, but in 1982 this was almost unheard of.

Reports came back from every location. Without a doubt, it must have been the single largest healing service in history at that time. It may still be.

I could not have imagined back there in 1967, when God called me to an international ministry, that a worldwide satellite would even exist. That was exceeding, abundantly above all we could think. But, thank God, it came to pass.

If ever there was a message worthy to share through *every* voice, it's the message of the blood covenant God offers to *us*.

Kenneth

"We Will Never Be the Same"

We had a wonderful meeting. The people came expecting, and they received the ministry. Many were healed. One man, who had been crippled, was running around the auditorium with his wife and daughter. None of us had words to express the feeling at the close.

D. H./Montgomery, Alabama

We had about 750 people in a room with a capacity of 500. We heard numerous comments from people saying they had never heard teaching on our covenant with God and on Communion like Brother Copeland gave. After the service, about 60 people asked for prayer, and one young woman who had never seen before received her sight.

J. W./Boise, Idaho

We had more than 200 persons— just about the capacity of our church— in attendance of the telecast, even

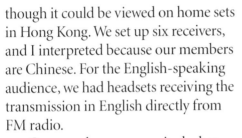

though it could be viewed on home sets in Hong Kong. We set up six receivers, and I interpreted because our members are Chinese. For the English-speaking audience, we had headsets receiving the transmission in English directly from FM radio.

Our people were so excited when they saw on the screens all of the believers in Fort Worth and in Seoul. The biggest church in Hong Kong is about 1,000 people, so our people had never seen that many believers in one place before. It made our people realize that they aren't part of some small...thing, but that they are members of the Body of Christ and we are worldwide.

D. B./Hong Kong

In South Africa, we held services in two main locations. In Johannesburg, the meeting was at Rhema Bible Training Center, and in Durban, we met in a theater. There were 3300 in Johannesburg and 1,000 in Durban. In addition there were scores and scores of

other small group meetings and even churches joining us at the same time to partake of Communion.

A number of people received salvation. Many received the Baptism in the Holy Spirit while they were prayed for right where they sat.

P. B./South Africa

In the Philippines, we were participating in the service at three sites. In Manila, we had 2300 people together laughing, crying, hollering, worshiping God and receiving healing. At the other two locations—one up in the mountains and the other on one of the southern islands—the people met and participated in the World Communion Service even though they did not have satellite reception.

The knowledge that we were receiving the body and blood of Jesus with believers all over the world really formed a tight bond of love between us.

P. S./Manila, Philippines

The World Communion Service was broadcast by satellite to locations all over the world.

When I began obeying God's command to preach the gospel through every available voice, I soon ran into a roadblock. I didn't like television. To me, it was about as close to nothing to do as you could get. I never enjoyed anyone putting a powder puff in my face. I didn't want anyone putting makeup on me. I didn't want someone sticking a camera in front of me. But we obeyed God and began televising our meetings, and from that we produced our Sunday broadcast. Then, after several years of weekly only broadcasting, the Lord began dealing with us about going on five more days a week—daily—six days a week! I did not want to do that. It was bad enough having cameras and all that went with them in our meetings. The daily programs would have to be made in a studio!

I wanted to preach to *people*, not to a red light and one big eye.

I didn't want anyone counting numbers in my face, telling me when to start and when to quit. I didn't like it. I didn't like anything about it.

"We're going to have to go on daily television next," Gloria mentioned one day.

"I'm not," I said.

"Yes, you are."

"I'm not going to do it." I *knew* I was going to have to do it, because God and I had been down that road over and over. I wanted to say "no" as long as I could, but it was futile. I couldn't get out of it without disobeying God.

When God first started talking to us about adding television to our ministry, I realized I had an even larger obstacle to overcome than not liking cameras, makeup, etc., added to our meetings.

I found out how much it would cost.

The people in television wrote the book on expensive.

I was lying across a hotel bed in Little Rock, Arkansas, one day, praying over the meeting we were having there, when the Lord began talking to me about television. I lay there praying in the spirit, but my mind was spinning.

How in the world can God ever get that kind of money to me? How can I ever get on television?

It was honest unbelief—if there is such a thing. The Lord will put up with it as long as you don't know any better, but there comes a time when He's heard enough. I'd reached that point, and He interrupted my thoughts.

Kenneth, don't seek ways to get money in. Seek ways to get the Word out. The money will then come in.

I knew that. But that afternoon a fresh revelation swept over me, and I realized that Jesus already knew exactly what He needed to do to get the money to me. Getting the money in wasn't my part of the arrangement. My part was preaching the Word.

Jesus, I realized, always had the hard part. I always had the easy part.

I figured I could endure the camera for Him.

Since He endured the Cross for me.

Kenneth

loria and I couldn't figure out how God was going to get us on television. We couldn't figure it out, so we stopped trying. Instead, we talked about it. We meditated on the Word. We discussed it. We didn't talk unbelief. We asked one another questions. We discussed our commission from God. We talked, and talked, and talked, and talked.

Then one weekend, we drove to Arkansas for a visit. On the way back home, we didn't have any more insight into how the ministry was going to be on television than we'd had a year before.

We stopped at Denny's to eat breakfast that morning. We sat down, ordered, prayed, ate...and started talking again about going on television. Suddenly something changed.

Snap. God's plan for our television ministry dropped in my heart, and snapped in place like a piece to a jigsaw puzzle. That quick!

I looked at Gloria and saw the same look on her face. I said, "Gloria, tomorrow is Monday. Let's go home and get on TV."

"Why don't we do that?"

It was the easiest-looking thing. We didn't have a crying dime, but we had faith. If you have faith, the dimes will be there, so who cares?

Why did the Lord drop it into place like that? Because we were operating in the kingdom of God, not the kingdom of the natural. I never thought, *Let's call the bank!*

They would have laughed, but God wasn't laughing.

I said, "OK."

Gloria said, "OK."

Jesus said, *OK, let's do it!*

We got home Monday and did it. Don't ask me how, because I still don't know how. But we went on television weekly in 1979, and we're still on today.

K e n n e t h

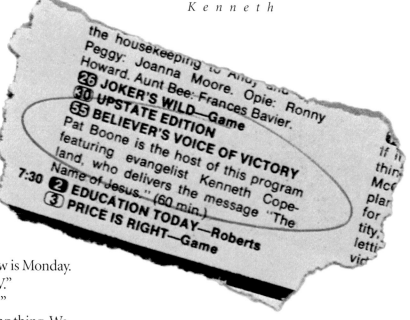

We were in Australia in February of 1988, when the Lord spoke to Gloria and me and gave us an assignment that turned out to be the largest step of faith this ministry had ever taken. He said, *As soon as you get back home, I want you to add a daily broadcast to your ministry. I want you to be on television, not one day a week, but six days a week.*

During that time, particularly in the United States, there was a lot of scandal surrounding TV ministries. The stock people took in television preachers was at an all-time low. I wasn't looking for ways to get *on* more television. I was looking for a way to get *off*.

The popularity of television preachers wasn't the only reason I didn't want to do it at that time. We had a million-dollar deficit on our weekly television program. We didn't have the money to go on daily television. We didn't have the personnel either. We had a few people on staff to help in television, but to produce a daily broadcast we needed a *lot* of people. Besides that, we didn't have the equipment. We rented what we needed to televise the meetings, but *rent* equipment for a daily broadcast? That's 260 programs a year.

When the Lord spoke to us about daily television, both of our heads spun around about twice. We had enough to do, and we weren't looking for any more.

This is a set where many of the television broadcasts are taped.

When we boarded the airplane to go home, I leaned back in my seat and argued with God the whole trip. "I don't want to do that," I said. "I'm already busy."

I didn't ask you what you wanted to do. I want you to get on daily television. And don't preach. Teach. Bring My people to a place of strength in this earth—because the Glory is coming.

Gloria sighed and said, "Oh, my." Then she started figuring and planning. I didn't bother, because I knew, naturally speaking, there wasn't any way. I just took hold of what God said, and hung onto it. Finally, something clicked inside of me and I didn't see any reason *not* to do it.

"Let's do it," I told Gloria.

"We don't have any money."

"That doesn't matter. We've got faith."

Gloria looked down at her figures. "Are we going to do it anyway?"

"Yeah."

Back in the early days she would have said, "Oh, dear Jesus."

Now she said, "Thank You, Jesus, because here we go!"

Over the years, a whole lot of her *practicality* had rubbed off on me. And a whole lot of my *jump* had rubbed off on her. We met one another in the middle. Now both of us are bold, and both of us are practical. Of course, that's what God wanted all along.

So how did we jump from weekly television to a daily broadcast?

By faith.

We meditated the Word. We confessed our success. We built our faith. We called those things that be not as though they were.

We did all the same things you'll have to do to reach your next faith goal.

We got out of the boat of our comfort and put our feet in the water.

We took one step at a time.

We didn't look at the wind.

We didn't look at the sea.

We didn't look at the bank account.

We looked to God.

As always, God was faithful to His Word.

Oh, by the way. That million-dollar deficit cleared up almost immediately. It pays to obey God.

Kenneth

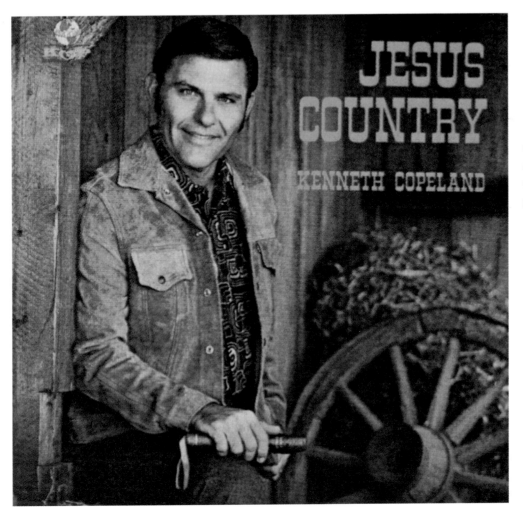

I can't remember a time in my life when music didn't play a part. There was a day, however, when singing became first place. It happened when I was in the fourth grade. I was standing next to my desk while we sang the national anthem. Suddenly, my teacher grabbed me by the arm and started toward the door. Before I knew what was happening, she was leading me down the hall.

My heart sank.

It wasn't the first time I'd been yanked to the principal's office.

But this time, I couldn't figure out for the life of me what I'd done wrong! And instead of taking me to the principal's office, she took me to her car.

Apparently she called my mother before she left, because my mother met us on our front porch when we drove up.

I could tell that Mama was just as worried as I was.

"Listen to this," my teacher instructed Mama. Then she sat down at our piano and started playing. Turning to me, she said, "Sing!"

I sang.

It was the first time in my life I'd been jerked out of a classroom for doing something *right!* While I sang, my teacher and Mama looked at me like they'd never seen me before.

I remember them talking about the depth and quality of my voice.

I thought *anybody* could do that.

From that point on, all I wanted to do was sing.

Actually, my desire to be a singer was one of the things that caused me to run from God. By the time I was a junior in high school, I knew God had a call on my life. That's *not* what I had in mind.

I recorded a song called "Pledge of Love" in 1957. That very *day,* I received my draft notice. The record was released while I was in basic training in the U.S. Army. It did real well, but I couldn't do anything about it. While that record was on the move, instead of being available to accept offers to perform on national TV *(The Steve Allen Show)* and movie soundtracks, etc., I stood guard duty or some other terrible thing. I'll tell you, I didn't know what to do. I couldn't understand it.

Today, I thank Almighty God for protecting me.

Two other young men had their first records on the charts at the same time "Pledge of Love" was. Their names were Johnny Mathis and Elvis Presley. That kind of success would have destroyed me.

Finally, about a year after I got out of the Army, I walked away from the 20 year dream of being an entertainer.

I didn't sing for a long time after I began this ministry. Why? I had a lot to *unlearn.* I knew how to entertain, and I knew how to sell a song.

That's not what I was called to do.

The call on my life is to preach the Word of God. I can do that with or without a melody, but the motive of my heart has to be that the Word goes forth. I'm not saying that there isn't an element of entertainment in ministry music. I am saying that it's wrong for someone with a call on their life to make entertainment a priority.

I had to unlearn entertaining, and learn to be led by the Holy Spirit.

There have been times when I was singing under a powerful anointing of God one moment, then slipped over into entertaining the next. The anointing lifted faster than I could form another note.

It's an awful thing to have happen.

I fully expect the same results when I sing as when I preach—with one added advantage.

The melody.

People don't mentally challenge words mixed with melody like they do the spoken word. You can listen to a song while you're doing something else mentally.

Music has the ability to transcend the human intellect. While that's a blessing, it's also what makes certain lyrics so dangerous. While music has the ability to calm the mind so that the heart can receive, there are some things you don't want your heart to hear.

I don't want to get out of balance

Kenneth singing at 1997 West Coast Believers' Convention, Anaheim, California.

where rhythm is concerned. About the time somebody says, "God could never use that," He'll make a fool out of you and use it.

Satan has never invented a rhythm, because there is no truth in him.

That surprises a lot of people. I'm convinced from the Word of God that he was the archangel of praise. But he didn't *invent* any of it. He has never originated anything. He's a perverter. He takes from God and perverts.

What you have to watch is the lyric content. People have said, "Oh, that's just horrible. I don't ever want to hear that old rock-and-roll stuff. I love this beautiful song." Then they'll sing something with a nice melody that is a slap in the face of Calvary.

We're just so footsore and poorly shod, but at the end of the journey is God.

We're *not* footsore or poorly shod! We're shod with the preparation of the gospel of peace. That's not poorly shod. Furthermore, I don't know about you, but I *started* this journey with God. He's been with me every step of the way. He's not only with me, He's in me, around me, behind me and over me.

I don't care how pretty a song is, you'd better watch the lyrics. A lot of them are totally doubt and unbelief.

We need to watch for the Word, whether we're preaching or singing. Whatever we're doing, if we're sitting down to eat, watch for the Word, and watch the words of our mouths.

A lot of things affect the anointing on music, not the least of which is our motive. When you get right down to it, Elvis Presley used to give people goose bumps. I'm not saying a whole lot of it was from the Holy Spirit, which is a shame, because there were times when the Spirit came on him. I've heard some of his gospel music that had an anointing on it.

Do you think Elvis was born again, Brother Copeland?

That's not my decision.

How could his music be anointed if he wasn't saved?

The same way I sang under the anointing before I was saved. The anointing of God came *on* me because of my Mama's prayers and the Word of God in certain songs I was singing. But that anointing wasn't *in* me until I gave my heart to the Lord Jesus.

Kenneth

Building a Debt-Free Ministry

Owe no man any thing, but to love one another:

for he that loveth another hath fulfilled the law. ROMANS 13:8

T he Lord let Gloria and me know from the beginning that we were to live our lives, and run this ministry, without going into debt. Yet, there I was on the go preaching, traveling from state to state in a car that was leaking from every joint. Only prayer got it from one place to another. But borrowing money to buy a new one was out of the question.

I knew that we had to believe God for money to buy a car, so Gloria and I set ourselves in agreement about it and prayed. We asked God for the money by October 30 of that year.

In the meantime, we faithfully thanked God for the answer. October arrived with no money in sight. Week after week passed, while we continued to believe that we had received.

I was in Omaha, Nebraska, on October 30. The day came and went with no money in sight. When I woke up October 31, my feelings were hurt and I was mad. *We agreed and we didn't get it!* I thought. *What's the matter? Doesn't God care?*

In effect, I was about to tell God that He missed it in Matthew 18:19 when He said, *"If two of you shall agree on earth as touching any thing that they shall ask,*

(Facing page)
"When we left Tulsa in 1968 and moved back to Fort Worth, Ken's dad's insurance office was in this building. A.W. gave us two small rooms and we shared a secretary."

—GLORIA

it shall be done for them of my Father which is in heaven." Of course, He didn't miss it, and before I could spew out all that doubt and unbelief, He interrupted me.

Is My Word any different today than it was yesterday? He asked.

"No."

Then why did you *change?*

"Because yesterday was the 30th."

What does that have to do with anything?

In that instant of time, I caught sight of the limitlessness of God. All of a sudden, I knew *God* didn't miss it. I knew His Word wasn't in error.

"Glory to God!" I shouted. "I won't let go! Thank You, Lord, I have that money by October 30!"

It was already October 31! All that day I confessed, "Yes, glory to God, I have it by the 30th. The Word of God is true, and Gloria and I agreed."

Finally Satan spoke up. *You can't do that!*

"I just did it, Sport!"

No, you can't! The 30th was yesterday!

"What do I care? I have it by the 30th."

The devil couldn't handle that kind of talk, so he ran away.

The next day, I was still preaching in Omaha, when I received an urgent phone call. The man said, "Oh, Brother Copeland, please forgive me. I just feel so bad about this. God spoke to me two weeks ago and told me to send you some money, but I didn't do it. I'm telling you, God got all

over me last night for putting that off."

It was there all the time! "I don't doubt it, Brother," I said. "Send it on over." He and I shouted and praised God together. Victory had come to us both.

If, on October 31, I had set aside the agreement that Gloria and I prayed in faith, I would have never seen a dime of what God had for me. I would have spewed doubt and unbelief all over the place, and God would have had no faith to work with in that situation. Not only that, but my Partner would have lost the opportunity to sow the seed to the victory God had planned for him. Wallowing around in unbelief is a very costly luxury no one can afford.

How many times have you had the devil, or even someone you respect, tell you, "You can't do that!" Those words are the words of the world.

Believing God for that car to keep going showed me the difference so clearly.

Hearing the Word of God, meditating the Word of God, and acting on the Word of God develops faith.

Hearing the word of the world, meditating on the word of the world, and acting on the word of the world develops fear.

The devil, all his demons and the whole world were still screaming, *You can't do that!* But Gloria and I weren't listening. We were heading out to preach the gospel...

Kenneth

I’ve learned that most of the time, we develop character in the midst of spiritual storms. The Bible said we should *"add to your faith virtue"* (2 Peter 1:5). If you translate the word "virtue," it means *moral energy*. It also means *heroism*, or *doing the heroic thing*.

I always thought John Wayne would have made a good preacher. The man had grit. It's too bad that Hollywood portrays most preachers as Brother Milky Toast.

Living by faith means that sometimes you have to walk up and spit in the devil's eye. If he dares you with one thing, take him down twice.

I was preaching someplace one time where the offerings were…conservative. It was the last day of my meeting, and I still needed $900 to meet my budget. The devil started pushing me about it.

You're not going to make it, he said. *This is the stingiest bunch in town, and you're not going to make the budget. You still have $900 to go, and you only have one service left. There's not $900 in this whole bunch!*

He chewed on me all afternoon. I had already learned that you can't fight thoughts with thoughts. You have to fight thoughts with words spoken aloud. So I left my hotel room and went outside where I could *talk*.

As long as I quoted scripture out loud, the devil didn't bother me. But the minute I hushed, he started yammering. Every time he started I'd say, "No, I rolled the care of the finances over onto God. My God always causes me to triumph in Christ Jesus, the Anointed One. Thank God, my seed is in the ground, and I believe I receive the harvest in Jesus' Name."

I'd get quiet just long enough to clear my throat and the devil would chime in. *You're never going to get that $900!*

Finally, I'd had enough.

"Shut up! If you keep talking to me like that, I'm not even going to *receive* an offering tonight. But God will get that $900 to me anyway, and I'll testify about it everywhere I go. Do you understand? If you don't shut up, you're going to make it worse on yourself!"

I meant every word of it.

About that time, a car came through the hotel gate with its horn honking. It came to a stop next to me, and a man rolled down the window and said, "Brother Copeland, I haven't missed a service up till now, and I'm not going to miss the whole service tonight, but I *am* going to miss the offering. I have another appointment, or I wouldn't even miss that. I'm just so glad I caught you, because I don't want to miss that offering."

He handed me a check.

It took a lot of training, but I never look at a check before I pray. What the flesh wants to do is grab that check, take a good look and say, "Oh, I'm going to pray a good prayer on this one!"

Other times you'd look at the check and say, "I'll tell you something, Hoss, you haven't got a prayer."

I don't look at checks before I pray, because that's somebody's seed and no matter what the amount, it's precious to God.

"God bless you, sir," I told the man, and we prayed over his check without my ever looking at it. When he drove away, I stood there and laughed at the devil.

I laughed real loud.

"You lying devil!"

I went back inside and looked at the check. *$500!*

We hadn't had a $500 offering the whole time I was there.

I would have lost that offering if I had let the devil keep putting pressure on me, because it's that kind of pressure that makes ministers put pressure on people.

I didn't put pressure on the people. I put pressure on the Word, then God directed that man to get that offering to me. (The balance of $400 did come in the offering that evening…to the penny!)

The devil tucked tail and ran.

I used that $900 to whip him again.

It was the "John Wayne" thing to do.

Kenneth

I preached a 21-day meeting for a pastor one time, and when it was over the man made a big deal about presenting me with a check for $250. This was supposed to be all the offerings received for 21 days twice a day. His people thought the check was for thousands of dollars. Basically, he'd robbed me of my offerings.

He didn't know it, but I'd walked in while he was praying one day. I kept quiet since he was in prayer for his church. "God, help us meet the bills for this church," he said. "If we don't meet the church bills during this meeting, we're finished."

If he'd been honest with me, I would have gotten in there and helped him believe God for the bills of that church. Instead, he lied and told the people during each offering that the entire offering was going to me. He didn't have to do that. We didn't have any kind of agreement concerning the offerings. He was pastor. He could have done whatever he saw fit with any offering he received. I didn't say anything about it, and preached the rest of the services. When the meeting closed, it was bad enough that he took my offerings, but he had to make a big presentation before the congregation. They had no idea that he was giving me $250.

How does one get by preaching 21 days for $11 a day when you had to drive there and back? I went in the hole financially on that meeting.

I tried to be nice. But I have to admit,

I got really bent out of shape after that last service and the great check presentation. I went to our room (we were staying in the pastor's home) and told Gloria, "I've been robbed!" Then a *mad* came all over me, and I started slipping. I thought, *Good heavens, if that man wanted to rob me, the least he could have done was not make a ceremony out of it.*

"I'll tell you what I'm going to do," I said to Gloria. "I'm going in there and thank him. I'm going to get him outside and spank him. Maybe I can whip another two or three hundred out of him."

"No, you're not," Gloria said.

"Yeah, I am, too."

"No, you're *not!*"

"Yeah…I'm going."

"Kenneth, you know good and well that's against the Word of God."

"I'll repent in the morning, but he stole my money and I don't like it."

Boy, she jumped in the middle of me. "You're acting worse than he did!"

She was right, and I had to repent. I repented to Gloria and to God.

The Word says to be angry and sin not (Ephesians 4:26). I got the "be angry" part, but I was having trouble with the "sin not."

"Kenneth," Gloria finally said, "if you keep this up, you're going to lose the budget of this meeting."

That stopped me. See, I thought I had *already* lost the budget. When Gloria said those words to me, I could see through

the devil's scheme. That meeting wasn't over until *I* said it was over! Jesus was still my Lord. He sent me to that church. I would believe *Him* for my budget. That pastor was His servant, not mine. The budget of that meeting was His budget, not mine.

I took my eyes off the problem and put them on the One Who sent me there. "I just roll the care of that budget over onto You, Lord," I prayed.

The pressure lifted off me. I drove down the road singing, happy…and broke.

We reached a little town in Louisiana by lunch and visited with a brother while we ate at a restaurant. We had a nice visit, and I never mentioned anything that happened. To say anything about it would be gossip, and we'd have to talk lack to do it. Our faith was on the line, so there was no way we could do that.

We had to be very careful what we ordered off the menu in that restaurant, so we held out and didn't eat anything else until we made it to Gloria's mother's house in Prescott, Arkansas. Thank God, she had supper fixed. She always does!

We hadn't been there long when the phone rang. "Kenneth," Mary said, "that

"Our office on University Drive wasn't glamorous, but it was bigger. Our staff had grown to seven! We moved into this office in November 1971, and had outgrown it when we moved out in November 1972."

— GLORIA

was the sheriff! He wanted to know if you were here!"

A little while later, the phone rang again, and it was the man we'd visited with at lunch. "Brother Copeland, I'm sorry, but I remembered you were headed to your mother-in-law's house, and I called the sheriff to track you down."

"Why, what's the problem?" I asked.

"While we were at lunch, the Lord told me to give you $500, and I didn't do it. I just sat there like a fool, and I'm asking you to forgive me. I knew I couldn't sleep tonight if I didn't tell you I'm sorry, and that the money is on its way."

That $500 more than took care of the rest of the budget.

When you put your faith on the line with God...

It's not over—until it's over.

Kenneth

According to the Bible, God wants us to be strong and of good courage. Do you know why? Because it takes courage to live a life of faith. As this ministry grew, I knew we were going to have to plant a lot of financial seed to stay out of debt. That meant we needed courage.

I'll never forget the time the Lord spoke to me and said, *Give Kenneth Hagin $50,000.* Hearing direction like that takes courage.

Especially when all you have is $50.

The only thing I knew to do was meditate on what God said until it seemed easy. When I first heard the Lord say that, it didn't seem easy at all.

It seemed impossible.

"How am I going to do that, Lord?" I asked. "I can't see any way!"

That was my problem, of course. I couldn't *see* it, because I hadn't developed

"Our Bolt Street office was the nicest one yet. We were here from November of 1972 to December of 1975. We grew to a staff of 12! When we moved out, this later became Jerry Savelle's ministry office (shown here)."
—GLORIA

spiritual vision for a $50,000 gift. So I started meditating on giving $50,000 to Brother Hagin.

Remember, I was meditating on the fact that I *could,* not on the fact that I *couldn't.* I never allowed myself to think, *I can't do that. Oh, I wish the Lord hadn't told me that. How in the world will I ever be able to give away $50,000?*

I began to think, *Glory to God! I'm going to give Brother Hagin $50,000!* Can you guess what happened when I began meditating on it?

I began to get tickled. I began to enjoy it. I became cheerful about it.

After a day or two, the Lord spoke again. *Don't wait until you have the entire $50,000! Start giving what you have now.*

I had $50.

I mailed Brother Hagin $50, and acted like it was $50,000.

When I did that, something happened, but not to my finances. Something happened to *me!*

I got so excited, I meditated on it day and night. Whenever I'd get a dollar or two in my pocket, I'd send it to Brother Hagin. If I had change after paying for a meal, I sent it to Brother Hagin. Sometimes I'd think of him and go buy him something.

I rat-holed nickels and dimes and dollars and sent it all to him. After a period of time, the very idea that I *wouldn't* give him $50,000 was ludicrous. I meditated on it until it looked like the simplest thing in the world. I got

caught up in it, and I enjoyed every minute of it.

One day the Lord said, *Why don't you call Buddy Harrison and see how your account is adding up?*

Now, Buddy (Brother Hagin's son-in-law) hadn't known what I was doing. The only people who knew were Gloria and Jesus. So I called Buddy and said, "Buddy, I'd appreciate it if you'd have

"This was the Bolt Street tape room. That's my younger sister, Jan (left), working on the mailing list."
— GLORIA

your accountant look up how much our contributions have been up to this point."

"OK," he said, "I'll call you back."

"You don't need to do that," I assured him. "Just drop me a note."

I'll never forget the day I got his letter. We'd given *more than $50,000!*

I was having such a good time, I passed the goal and didn't even know it.

That was good seed, and we needed to plant a lot of seed in good soil to grow a debt-free ministry.

Eventually there came a time when I could write a single check for $50,000. Of course, by then I was believing to give a quarter of a million dollars.

How did I meet that goal?

The same way. I started right where I was, and I meditated on it until it seemed like the simplest thing in the world. Sure enough, one day it was.

Kenneth

financially, things began to go better and better as the ministry grew. Then in 1984, something startling happened. We found ourselves $1 million in the red. I'll never forget it. Bills were coming at us from every direction, but on the income side, someone had turned off the faucet. When I began to pray about it, I didn't get any response from the Lord.

That was as much a red flag as the deficit. I knew enough about God to know He wasn't ignoring me. Something was wrong—a million dollars wrong—and it wasn't on God's end of the deal.

I'd learned over the years that if I had a problem with my physical body, the answer wasn't necessarily to jump up all of a sudden and pray healing. Instead, I would go to the Word and seek the wisdom of God as James 1:1-5 directs. Sometimes there were things that needed to be dealt with that didn't have anything

(Top) This was how the property at Lake Arlington looked before KCM moved there in 1975. (Bottom) The Lake Arlington property after renovations.

to do with sickness and disease. One thing is certain. God is never the problem. He is the Deliverer.

This wasn't a physical illness, but a million-dollar deficit is a very serious financial illness. So, I set everything aside and began to fast and pray. After about three days, I said, "Lord, I've been here three days and I need to hear from You about this. I need a million dollars."

The Spirit of the Lord answered me immediately. *You don't need a million dollars.*

"You could've fooled me!" I said. "Look at all these bills. It looks to me like I need a million dollars."

No, I could give you a million dollars, He said, *but in a few days you'd be right*

back in the same mess you're in now.

"Why, Lord?"

Because you have some spiritual problems in your ministry and in your own life. Until you correct them, these financial problems will stay with you.

He showed me that I'd made some wrong decisions and had been disobedient about some things a long time before that, and was now reaping the fruit of it. I repented and made some adjustments in my heart and mind. But I knew there was more to it than that. "What else do I need to do, Lord?" I asked.

Begin giving the top 10 percent of this ministry's income to help Jesus minister to others—especially the poor.

When you're faced with a million-dollar shortfall, the idea of giving more money seems ludicrous. But the fact is, the money I needed was a side issue— not the root problem. The root of the matter was ministry to the poor. Even if we'd found the money to pay off the deficit, we still would have had the problem, because some things were out of order.

So I did what, in the natural, appeared to be a foolish thing. In my hour of greatest financial need, I decided to give more than ever before.

What happened?

The faucet of finance began flowing freely again. And sure enough, I found out I didn't need a million dollars. I was fully supplied!

Kenneth

"This is a view of the Arlington lake property *before* we added five offices. The Lord really began to multiply this ministry while we were here. In 1975, we had a staff of 12. When we moved out in 1980, our staff had grown to almost 100!"
— GLORIA

The reason we must have the *force* of faith in our lives is to offset the *pressure* of this world. We'll need the force of faith to combat the pressure of the world as long as we live on this earth.

The need for faith never diminishes. On the contrary, Gloria and I have discovered that as our faith in God has grown, so have the opposing pressures. For example, not long after we began airing our daily TV broadcasts, we found ourselves with a deficit of more than $5 million dollars. Talk about pressure! People came into my office and said, "What are we going to do?"

"About what?" I asked.

"We're $5.75 million dollars behind. Are you going to get out there and tell the people about it?" These people weren't on my staff. My staff know better than to ask questions like that.

"You get on that mailing list," they continued, "and tell those people that if they don't give, you're going to take the television broadcast off the air."

The Eagle Mountain property as it looked in 1979. During World War II and for almost 20 years after the war, the property was used to train military troops. Since KCM moved there, the Lord now uses it to train His spiritual army!

"I'm not going to do that!" I said.

"Why not?"

"Because it's a lie! They'll carry me out of here with my toes sticking up before I'll ever do a thing like that."

You know, that few hundred dollars I needed in 1967 for tuition at ORU was as big a hurdle *then* as almost $6 million is *now*. I look at both needs the same way. Either the Lord can handle it, or He can't. Either the Bible is true, or it isn't.

When the Lord called me to this ministry 30 years ago, I told Him, "All I'm going to do is preach the Word, and tell people what happens to me. If You don't take care of me financially, I'll tell them that."

That's fair enough, the Lord said.

After all this time, I can honestly say that He *has* more than met *all* my needs.

So when I came up against that $5.75 million deficit, I had the sense to know that I had created a bottleneck somewhere. "Lord," I prayed, "I've messed up somewhere, and I don't know where the bottleneck is. So I'm going to sell off a bunch of land and equipment."

What will you sell next month? He asked.

Once again, God was telling me the problem was in the spirit and not in the natural. I knew I had seed in the ground, but *something* was messing up my harvest.

I wrestled with that problem for months. But I didn't make any headway until the night before our yearly Board of Directors meeting. I'd been dreading that meeting because I was going to have to stand up there and tell them about that deficit. I didn't know if they'd run me off, but I sort of hoped they would!

Each year in preparation for that meeting, all of our department heads make up their annual reports. Then the general overseer takes them and makes a report concerning the state of the entire ministry. Afterward, I present the report to the board.

It was midnight the night before the board meeting, and I hadn't even looked at the report. I knew the bottom line was a $5.75 million deficit. That was bad! Finally, I thought, *Well, I guess I'd better read through this thing. How ridiculous, to come this far and then flop!*

I started reading about our correspondence—it was the best year we'd ever had! I read about the tape ministry—it was the best year we'd ever had! I read about books—the best year! I read about the *Believer's Voice of Victory* magazine—its best year!

Every department was in the black!

I turned the page and stared at the report.

Overall, approximately 3.6 million souls came to Jesus this year!

I'd had the best year of my entire ministry, and I hadn't known it!

I turned to the television department. There it was—an almost $6 million black hole.

"Gloria," I said, "come here. Look,

every department in this ministry has had its best year—until you get to television. I wonder what the problem is with television?" She picked it up and started reading.

The Spirit of the Lord spoke up inside me, *The only department that got in trouble is the one you tried to carry. You rolled all the care of the other departments over onto Me, and I took care of them. Why don't you roll the care of that one over on Me, and I'll take care of it too?*

"Gloria!" I almost shouted, "I know what we did wrong!"

We picked up the Bible and turned to 1 Peter 5:6-7, *"Humble yourselves therefore under the mighty hand of God, that he may exalt you in due time: Casting all your care upon him; for he careth for you."*

I thought I'd learned that lesson years before in Beaumont, Texas, but here I was trying to carry responsibility for the television department. Gloria and I repented before the Lord. Then, together, we rolled the care of the entire television ministry over onto God. By faith we determined not to touch it with our thoughts, $900 or $6 million. Faith is faith, and thoughts are brought under authority by God's Word spoken aloud.

A few months later, that deficit was paid. What's more, we've been paying our television bills on time ever since. When it comes to our television department, the devil is the one feeling the pressure now!

Kenneth

Since 1986, Kenneth Copeland Ministries' International Headquarters has been located at Eagle Mountain near Fort Worth, Texas.

Ministry Is a Family Affair

Thy wife shall be as a fruitful vine by the sides of thine house: thy children like olive plants round about thy table. PSALM 128:3

Someone told me they wished they had my job at the ministry. I laughed and told them my job actually began when Gloria was born. My primary job then, and now, is being Gloria's mother. It's a job I'm honored to have.

Gloria was the firstborn of my seven children, and because there were always so many chores to do, we learned to work together easily when she was just a little girl. Later, when she was older and wanted me to sew her a new dress, I knew I could stop everything and make it because Gloria knew what needed to be done, and

she'd step in and do it. I never dreamed that the relationship we had then was preparation for me to help her in ministry.

I certainly wasn't prepared for a life in ministry the way some people are. We went to church, but not very often.

When I was just a girl of 12, an evangelist came to town and built a brush arbor on a vacant lot a couple of blocks from our house.

I walked down there by myself to see what was going on. Curious, I took a seat on the back row. When the minister gave an altar call, with fear and trembling I went forward and made Jesus Lord of my life.

For a number of years afterward, I

(Facing page) 1993, Kenneth and Gloria with their children and grand-children.

couldn't say I knew God well at all, but *He* knew *me*. He watched over me and kept me safe for the job He had for me to do. Gloria was saved in the late '60s, and that was just the beginning of the blessings and changes the Lord had in store for me, my children and my children's children.

I wasn't really surprised when Gloria and Kenneth went into the ministry. I saw it coming. While they lived in Little Rock, she often wrote me letters and they really ministered to me. She put her heart on those pages. She had such a heart to reach the unsaved and for Kenneth to preach the Word of God to the people. She really cared about people.

When I read her letters, it would come to my mind about that brush arbor meeting...I would remember the decision I had made to give my life to Jesus. I hadn't thought about it much until then, but I guess He had. The Lord doesn't forget.

As Kenneth and Gloria went into the ministry full time, and began preaching, God began instructing Gloria in a new direction. That caused my life to take a big turn. The Lord called her to teach the Healing Schools.

"Mother," she said, "I can't do this unless I have you to help me."

The children were young, and she needed someone to stay with them while she traveled. That was certainly one job I was qualified to handle.

I had never imagined my life outside of Center Point, Arkansas. But I packed up and moved to Fort Worth to help Kenneth and Gloria. I still had three of my own children at home, and now I was going to help keep Kellie and John. It was a decision I've never regretted.

The ministry office was on University Drive back then, and that's where I went to work as secretary. The entire staff consisted of six people. When Kenneth and Gloria were on the road, I went in early and was home before the children came home from school.

It seems hard to believe that it's been almost 30 years since I moved here to Texas. My children, and Gloria's, are grown. All totaled, I have 23 grandchildren and great-grandchildren. I know there are a lot of little ministers in the group. I can feel it.

Looking back, it's amazing what God has done in this family through the work He started in Kenneth and Gloria's hearts. He didn't just change them—He changed all of us. Kenneth didn't have any brothers or sisters, so he just embraced Gloria's as his own. He's been so wonderful. We aren't Kenneth's family and Gloria's family. We're just family.

I'm proud of Gloria when she preaches and teaches. I'm proud of her part in this ministry. But I'm equally proud of the way she raised her children. She has always been a good mother.

Whenever I go to one of the conventions, I always stand up at least once and look around at the thousands of people who attend. The Lord has brought this ministry, and all of us who work in it, a long way.

My job at the ministry is to take care of the gifts that are sent personally to Kenneth and Gloria. In addition, I still help Gloria. I've often joked about having doctor's hours. I'm on call. I try to have things ready for them whenever they get in—day or night.

Sometimes I hear they're coming in one day, but things get delayed and they don't make it in until the next day. They'll walk in the house and find a pot of soup on the stove. They look at one another and guess, "Did she put this on the stove yesterday, or did she do it today?"

I'm easily motivated to serve them, because that's what God has called me to do. They don't ask me to do a lot. Most of the time, I just see a need and fill it.

When I think about what God has done in this family, I start to cry. I am so very, very grateful for the goodness of the Lord!

Mary Neece

George and Terri
Pearsons with their
children, Jeremy
and Aubrey

One of my earliest memories was being a conspirator with my grandmother Vinita, whom I called "Nonnie." When I was just a little girl, she used to say to me, "Come on, Terri. Let's pray for your daddy now." I'd kneel down on the floor next to her and we'd weep and pray for him together.

Before he was saved, Daddy gave her a photograph of himself holding a cigarette. Instead of just framing the picture, or putting it in a photo album, Nonnie made 100 copies and mailed them to prayer groups across the country.

He never had a chance.

When I was 5 years old, I was on the *Romper Room* television show. I distinctly remember looking up at the cameras, and the people behind them, thinking, *That's what I want to do when I grow up.*

By the time I was 10, Daddy was born again and in the ministry. Although I was still in elementary school at the time, I started making big plans. I decided, *I'm going to go to school at ORU. Then I'll go to work with Daddy and travel with him.*

Back then, those two dreams seemed incongruous. We weren't thinking about television in those days. Daddy was busy making radio tapes. He used to sit in a chair inside a storage closet recording them. I sat on a brown footstool beside him, holding the stopwatch.

Those early years in ministry were exciting. I remember the time we rented a metal building at the fairgrounds in Lubbock, Texas. We'd been there for days, and nobody was coming to the meetings. Daddy decided to go house to house in a poor section of town not far from the fairgrounds. We split up in teams and began knocking on doors.

"Is there anybody here who needs prayer?" we said, inviting them to the meetings.

One woman came out of her house to go with us. She wore an apron over her dress, and a big straw hat. We were walking down an unpaved road when she asked, "You boys Pentecost?"

"Yes, Ma'am, we are," Daddy said.

That really bothered me, so I pulled on Daddy's coat. "I thought we didn't have a denomination."

"We don't," he said, "that means we speak in tongues."

"Oh…"

We had an outdoor rally during that meeting even though it was summertime and the temperature was over 100 degrees. I still remember one woman in particular who attended. She was legally blind. Daddy poured oil on her, and prayed. It was the first time I ever saw anyone jerk and dance around. Daddy said he didn't know if it was the Holy Ghost or that 100-degree oil.

It must have been the Holy Ghost, because God healed her eyes.

Then someone brought a baby with clubfeet. Daddy prayed, and the baby's

Terri—taking care of business.

feet turned in his hand! They were perfectly healed.

God healed a blind woman and a clubfooted baby.

After that, we had ourselves a meeting!

Another time, we went to Wichita Falls, Texas, in the dead of winter. It was snowing and bitterly cold. Daddy rented an abandoned drugstore that was in awful condition. They had to do a lot of work just to hold a meeting there. After a few days I got really upset. I didn't feel good, and I remember being very teary. I told Daddy how I was feeling, and asked, "What's the matter with me?"

He sat down and explained some things. "Well, you're sleeping on a couch," he said, "but even more important, you're in the middle of a lot of spiritual activity."

So this is spiritual!

That gave me a lot to think about.

You'd think that the small meetings would have been easier, but they weren't. There were a lot of tests in doing them.

When I was 12 years old, we were in Shreveport, Louisiana, for a meeting when God spoke to me about the call on my life to teach. I was wearing a little coral jumper with a blue and white polka-dot blouse. I guess only a woman would remember what she was wearing when God called her to teach. But I knew even at that age that saying "yes" to God was a moment to remember.

I'm glad that moment was frozen in time for me, because I had to hang onto it for years before it came to pass. After high school, I did what I'd been planning on doing since I was 10. I moved to Tulsa and enrolled at ORU.

I studied television broadcasting and learned a lot of things I would need to know in the years to come, but that wasn't God's only reason for sending me there. He also wanted me to meet a fellow student named George Pearsons.

I not only met him—I fell in love with him.

After George asked me to marry him, I took him home to meet the family. We finished out that school year, then Daddy asked George to come work and start the art department that summer. One weekend Daddy told George, "I believe the Lord wants you to stay. I need you right now. Why don't you pray about it?"

They kept George in Fort Worth but sent me back!

While I was still in school, I got it in my spirit that we were going to do television. I called Daddy from ORU all excited. "Let's go on television!"

Daddy said, *"No! It's not time."* He was *not* excited about that idea.

At the end of that year, I left ORU and went to work in the mail room at Kenneth Copeland Ministries. My only creative outlets were the occasional editing for the monthly newsletter, some nighttime DJ work at the local Christian radio station and the ministry softball team. TV looked forever away. I was in a store buying a softball glove, when I was tracked down by someone from the ministry.

"Have you heard?" she asked.

"Heard what?"

"Your dad called. We're going on *television!*"

I jumped, screamed and yelled all the way to my car.

I may not have been so excited if I'd realized then what a big job we had ahead of us. Nobody was doing weekly Christian television on a national level then like we're doing it now. There was no guarantee of an audience interested in watching our kind of ministry for an hour. In addition, we were working with hardly any money.

It was bad enough for Daddy to have to wear television makeup and have his face powdered. But he also had to bear

with us as we learned how God—not everyone else—wanted our broadcast to be done.

It would have helped us a lot if we could have started with a Christian television crew. But finding a Christian crew in those days was next to impossible. The few who existed were already working. So we forged ahead without one.

When we were in El Paso, Texas, doing our third TV taping, however, Daddy called me into the dressing room. "You get

Terri Pearsons,
Kellie Copeland and
Vinita Copeland

me a Christian crew or we're shutting this down now," he said. "I won't do this again."

He was asking for a miracle.

Thankfully, we knew that God was in the miracle business.

Even after we found a Christian crew, we felt like we were swimming upstream. The reason was, our approach to television was just the opposite of what was being taught back then. Nobody was teaching "Protect the Anointing" in college.

I fought the mind-set most professionals had about "religious" TV. In fact, I wanted to be as *un*religious as possible. I decided early on that we weren't going to shove cameras in Kenneth's and Gloria's faces. We weren't going to disturb the people in the meeting. We never exploited crying people in the congregation by focusing the cameras on them.

It was a challenge to work that way. But we knew that there was no point in Christian television unless we protected the anointing.

In the midst of all that, God reminded me that I was called to teach.

I started teaching the crew. I taught them spiritually, night by night, to get them focused on what we were doing, and why we were doing it.

Teaching made the difference.

Little did I know during all those years in television that the Lord was growing me up with the ministry. Today, George and I pastor Eagle Mountain International Church, and I'm fulfilling the call God put in my heart back in Shreveport, Louisiana, when I was 12.

I've come a long way since then. But I see now that whether it was holding the stopwatch for Daddy, reading the letters that flooded the mail room, helping with the radio broadcast, handling television broadcasts or pastoring a church—our ministry has always been about one thing.

Lives.

It's about blind eyes seeing, and club-footed children running.

And the only thing that changes lives is the Anointed One and His Anointing.

Today, like then…it's all about *Jesus*.

*Terri
Copeland
Pearsons*

y dad was the production manager of a major art studio in New York City who worked with magazines like *Life* and *Time* while I was growing up. I was a second-year art student in Boston when I made Jesus the Lord of my life. Two years later, I was so hungry for God that I left my home in Massachusetts and moved to Tulsa, Oklahoma, to study at Oral Roberts University. I wanted to become a pastor.

I felt like I'd arrived in heaven when I landed on the ORU campus in the fall of 1975. There was always something happening—concerts, television tapings or notable Christian figures—the Word was going forth somewhere all the time. I heard the Gaithers, Second Chapter of Acts, Corrie ten Boom, Kathryn Kuhlman and, of course, Oral Roberts. Spiritually, Tulsa was the place to be.

ORU's version of sororities and fraternities is "brother and sister wings." Each wing from a male dorm was matched to a wing from a female dorm for social purposes. I met a girl on my sister wing named Terri Copeland.

We were about as different as Texas and Massachusetts.

Toward the end of September, I heard that Terri's father was going to preach at one of Brother Hagin's meetings. I was torn. I wanted to go, but I *had* to settle down and spend more time studying.

I'll go this one last time, I decided. *Afterward, I'll stop trying to attend all the campus events.*

Brother Copeland hadn't been speaking long before he said, "One of the greatest honors of a man of God is to be loved and admired by a woman of God."

That's what I want!

A while later he added, "One of the greatest things a man of God can do in prayer is pray in other tongues."

The impact of those words on my life were so great I felt like he had turned around and pointed at me.

I wasn't Spirit-filled.

A.W. and Vinita Copeland with George Pearsons

That night, I went back to my dorm room and asked God to fill me with His Holy Spirit.

He did.

A couple of weeks later, our brother and sister wings went on a retreat.

It was there, away from the hustle and bustle of campus life that Terri and I really got to know one another. Terri came home with me to Massachusetts during Christmas break, and I proposed.

She accepted.

God had given me both of the things Brother Copeland spoke about that night in Tulsa. The ability to pray in tongues and to be admired and loved by a woman of God.

We left my family and flew to Texas so that I could get to know Terri's.

"I really want to be a man of God," I told Kenneth.

"I'll send you my Bible course," he said.

We'd been back in school a few days when someone from the post office phoned. "Please come pick up your boxes."

Boxes?

I arrived at the post office and found three huge boxes addressed to me. Inside was every tape series that Brother Copeland had preached. I pulled the first series out of the box. It was *Integrity of God's Word.*

I sat down and listened to the series, taking notes.

Then I pulled out the next set of tapes. And the next.

I didn't have time for all those concerts now. The Word of God was *transforming* me.

To show my appreciation for the tapes, I designed a new ministry logo and sent it to Brother Copeland. When we finished that school year, he asked me to come to Fort Worth and start the ministry's art department.

What I thought would be a summer job has now stretched into 21 years.

Terri and I were fasting and praying one Saturday that summer when Brother Copeland asked me to stay with the ministry full time. I prayed and agreed to stay. Terri flew back to Tulsa.

The next few months were some of the most difficult of my life.

What have I done? I asked myself over and over. I left the place where Kathryn Kuhlman held one of her last services, a place where something was always happening, to move to a Texas town and work for a tiny ministry. And Terri was back at school—without me.

I reminded myself that I had never set out to follow either events or people. I set out to follow God and God had planted me *here.*

In addition to running the art department, I traveled with Kenneth every other week for three-day meetings. I was living with A.W. and Vinita Copeland during that time, and helping Vinita with her Bible class. When I started the art department, I set my faith for a product

that was even better than the best of the secular world.

I believed God to transmit the anointing through art.

The following year, I inherited the publications department. I believed God to transmit the anointing through the written word.

When Terri came back from ORU later that year, God fulfilled her desire to get the Word of God out through the medium of television. I helped her fulfill that dream.

My dream of pastoring a church had been on the shelf so long I almost forgot about it. Then, in 1988, when I was appointed Executive Director of Kenneth Copeland Ministries, the Lord resurrected it. *I want you to pastor the staff,* He said.

Pastor the staff. That gave me a lot to think about. When I first joined the ranks of Kenneth Copeland Ministries, the staff numbered 13. Now they'd grown to a rather large flock which God called me to shepherd.

It was no small thing to me that God would entrust those people to my care. I didn't take the responsibility lightly, but as in everything I'd done, I tried to pass Kenneth's and Gloria's hearts along to the people.

I'd been "pastoring" as Executive Director for five years in 1993, when the position as pastor of Eagle Mountain International Church became available. I'd been stepping in and filling voids in this ministry. But I didn't want to just fill a void at Eagle Mountain.

I had to fulfill a call.

Kenneth and Gloria had spent 18 years fathering me in the faith and imparting to me what they had learned. Now, it was my turn to father. I had so much in me that needed to be given to others. If I didn't, I thought I would pop!

I went to Kenneth and Gloria. "I *must* pastor Eagle Mountain International Church," I said. They were concerned.

"How can you handle the Executive Director position *and* pastor the church? That load is too heavy."

"I can do them both until John is ready to step in as Executive Director," I assured them. "Pray about it and see what the Lord says."

The Lord said, *"Yes!"*

In 1993, I stepped into the call to

George and Terri
Pearsons

which the Lord had been preparing me. For the next two and a half years, until August 1995, I continued in my position as Executive Director. Then, when John moved into the Executive Director position, I was free to pastor full time.

Looking back over the past 21 years, I clearly see the path I've followed. It was as though the Lord said, *OK, learn to express the anointing through art. Learn to express the anointing through the written word. Learn to express the anointing through administration.* **Now, express the anointing through the spoken word.**

The Lord spoke to me prophetically at the 1994 Southwest Believers' Convention through Jerry Savelle. "George...in your heart you have carried an image from a photograph that has been very dear to you," he said. "And you've said

regarding that photo, 'Lord, I wish You'd trust me with that kind of anointing like You did Brother Roberts and Brother Copeland.' Well, the Lord says He trusts you, George!"

I knew exactly what he was talking about, even though Brother Savelle had never been in my office. I have two photos in my office that are very dear to me. The first is a picture of the hungry, 30-year-old student Kenneth Copeland watching intently as Oral Roberts ministered to a woman in a wheelchair in 1967. The second is a photo of me, nine years later, standing beside Kenneth Copeland and studying him with the same intensity as he ministered to a man in a wheelchair.

Both Oral Roberts and Kenneth Copeland are dear to me. But God knows that isn't why those pictures hold such a place in my heart.

They represent spiritual hunger. The hunger that drove me to leave my home in Massachusetts. I couldn't have put a name to it when I was 22 years old.

I just knew I was hungry for God.

Now I know I was hungry for the yoke-destroying, burden-removing power of God. The power that raised Lazarus out of his tomb. The same power that raises people out of wheelchairs.

Those pictures keep me spiritually hungry...for the *anointing*.

George Pearsons

M y earliest memories are of our little house in Tulsa. I was 3 years old when I saw an angel there. When I described him to my parents, I said, "He had a king-thing."

That meant crown.

"And he looked like Mr. Clean."

When Daddy left ORU and started traveling, the whole family went with him as often as we could. When I started grade school, we traveled with a tutor. I thought it was great fun, because I had friends *everywhere*.

When I was in the second grade, I started having trouble with reading. My teacher told my parents, and Daddy had a talk with me. "I want you to start saying something," he said.

Win and Kellie Kutz with their children, (left to right): Max, Lyndsey, Rachel and Jenny

Kellie—the best reader in Fort Worth.

contrary to their prayers came out their mouths. Whenever I asked for something, Daddy would say, "That sounds like a good faith project." Then he'd help me believe for it.

He didn't just preach integrity in the pulpit and not live it at home, either. It's hard to explain, but Daddy was always there for us, even when he was gone. If he said he was going to do something, he *did* it.

I remember one time when I wanted a new bicycle.

"I have to pedal 90 miles an hour to keep up with the others," I complained. Besides, the new bikes had *banana seats.*

Daddy figured out that my bicycle needed a new sprocket.

He spent one whole night in the garage. The next morning I woke up and didn't recognize my bike. It had a new sprocket that let me keep up with my friends. It had a brand new banana seat. And *streamers!*

I realize now that he spent all night in the garage because his schedule was so hectic that he didn't have any other time to do it. But in ministering to others, he never failed to love and serve us.

Even though our lives were hectic, and Daddy was gone a lot, my mother never seemed to lose her patience with us. Since then she has become well known for her teaching on the fruit of the spirit. What very few people know is that for years before she *taught* on the fruit of the

"What?" I asked, curious.

"I want you to say, 'I'm the *best* reader in Fort Worth.'"

It worked. The more I said it, the more I believed it. Before long, my reading skills matched my confession. Reading became fun for me, and I still love to read.

When I started in third grade, we stopped traveling with a tutor and settled down to school life in Fort Worth. Mother stayed home with us most of the time while Daddy traveled.

I never remember my parents telling me we couldn't afford something. Looking back as an adult, it's clear that they were having to believe for *everything*. Yet nothing spirit, she *exhibited* that fruit in the most trying of circumstances. John and I were her proving ground, and we were good at what we did. When we were children, we did *not* provoke one another to love.

But we certainly provoked one another.

Through all our fights, bickering and the pressure of a growing ministry, she was *always* calm, patient and peaceful. Don't misunderstand, she was never a wimp. She always stood her ground, but she didn't lose her patience.

My mother, more than anyone else, has always represented the Holy Spirit to me.

I remember one summer she was outside working in her garden when John and I got into a fight. She listened to us for a minute, sighed and went to get two sacks.

Back outside, she handed one to each of us.

"I want each of you to pick up all the rocks you can find in the yard and put them in these bags."

There were a *lot* of rocks in that yard!

She was an expert at diverting our anger and getting us involved in something constructive.

She has always been a hard worker, too. I still remember the sight of that old house we got in Arkansas. It was falling apart and looked awful. I was shocked that anyone could see any hope for it.

My mother did. She said it had "potential." She could look past the walls papered with newspaper. She could look past the labor it would take. I never knew anyone to work as hard as she did fixing up that house.

Another thing she mastered was the fine line of being a good friend to her children while still being their mother. The friendship she nurtured between us has grown and matured over the years. Today, she is still my best friend. I'd rather spend time with her than do anything else.

Our family life took a big shift when I was around 13 years old. That's when God called Mother to minister alongside Daddy. We went from having one parent home to having both of them gone a lot. My grandmother "Ma Dear" stayed with us. That year, I got an idea.

I'd never heard of anyone doing it, and I never heard a sermon on the subject, but I had a deep revelation about sowing and reaping. I *knew* I couldn't out-give God.

I remember going to my bedroom, shutting the door and praying.

"Father, I'm *giving* my parents to You for Your service. I believe that I receive a hundredfold return."

I believe that prayer obligated God in ways I'll never understand.

I didn't suffer because of their ministry, or because of the time we spent apart. Somehow, God made what they were called to do so big in my heart that I was excited to be a part of it.

They were preaching in Charlotte the day I graduated from high school. That would have been a painful thing for a lot

Kellie sings with
Kenneth in one of
the meetings.

of kids, but it didn't bother me. I think it was God's grace working in me because I had given them to Him.

I graduated on a Friday night, and there were parties all weekend. None of that mattered to me. Graduation paled in comparison to what God was doing in Charlotte. I didn't need my parents in Fort Worth because my heart was in that meeting! I hated to miss *anything* God

was doing. Their meeting was over Saturday night, but in spite of that, they gave me the most wonderful graduation gift.

They flew me to Charlotte for the last day of the meeting.

There was literally no place on earth I would have rather been.

One of the reasons this ministry is a family affair is because my parents never waited for us to grow up and become

valuable before they got us involved. They esteemed us as valuable because, to them, we *were*.

Daddy must have sensed early that one day I would have a music ministry. He didn't wait until I became proficient before he asked me to sing at his meetings. I stood up there and sang while my voice croaked and cracked.

The result is that I never felt like there was *anything* I couldn't do. I sang two songs on one of Daddy's albums when I was 15. I recorded my first album, *Refreshing Times,* when I was 18.

In addition to the music albums, I started my Superkids' project, which to date includes three music/adventure cassettes and three videos.

I was only 12 years old when God called me to minister to children.

There are things the Lord told Mother and Daddy to do that are being fulfilled through their children and our spouses. When God told them that they would have a ministry center and pray for the sick every day, I know they must have wondered, *How?*

Today, we know the answer to that question is George and Terri.

Daddy has always had a heart for children. He never puts children on a back burner. Yet, many of the things God called him to do for children are being fulfilled in me. And Win helps Daddy with his music.

The same is true for John and Marty. As Executive Director of the ministry, John is fulfilling part of their call. And Marty keeps us in shape.

My parents didn't have a manual on how to raise their children by faith. But they still managed to pass their heritage along to us. Now, they are helping us instill the same love and faith in *our* children, Rachel, Jenny, Lyndsey and Max. My children are so much further in the Lord now than I was at their ages because they are getting the benefit of two generations.

As a parent, there is nothing as satisfying as seeing my own children walk by faith, walk in love, give, and pray for the sick.

What a heritage!

The ministry of the Holy Spirit that so flows through my mother is expressed in my ministry because all that she is, she instilled in me. And I watched her live by the Holy Spirit every day.

I, like the rest of the family, can minister with Daddy's heart because I am *of* my father, Kenneth Copeland.

Because he represented a loving father so well, today I have a deeper understanding of my loving Heavenly Father. I have a deep revelation that I am *of* Him.

Kellie
Copeland
Kutz

When I was a young boy growing up in Seattle, Washington, I used to watch jets take off and land from nearby Boeing Field. How I wanted to fly! I could imagine the powerful thrust of a jet engine as it soared into the heavens. Airplanes were my primary connection with heaven in those days. I went to church with my parents, but never made Jesus the Lord of my life.

As I grew older, music and engineering competed with flying for my interest. In time, I graduated from the University of Washington with a degree in electrical engineering. I also played electric bass in a band.

Where is this taking me? I wondered. I didn't want to spend my life as an engineer at Boeing as so many others did. Neither did I want to be 60 years old playing in a band at the Elk's Club.

A year after I graduated, I stumbled onto a recording studio in Seattle that, for me, was like visiting a *Star Trek* set. The studio, owned by actor Danny Kaye, was unlike any I'd ever seen.

This is a perfect combination of music and engineering! I thought, looking at their $2 million recording complex.

I filled out a job application.

One month later, they offered me a position—answering the phones, at night, for $2.25 an hour.

It wasn't exactly what I had in mind. I wrestled about whether to take the job, or go find a position better suited to my degree. In the end, I took the job.

My first night at the studio, I met rock star Steve Miller, whose music included the hit, "Fly Like An Eagle." I decided the job had possibilities.

Two years later, I worked as an engineer with Steve on two of his new records. Together they sold 9 million copies.

Two years after that, I was promoted to manager of the studio.

In the intervening years, I'd become the studio's biggest client. I worked with musicians like Mike Deasy on a recording

In addition to leading the band and running the music department, Win Kutz is also a pilot for the ministry.

for Bo Diddley. Mike was a guitarist who'd played with Elvis and the Beach Boys. I also worked with artists like Johnny Mathis, The Spinners and Heart.

While I was managing the studio, I also fulfilled a two-year contract as a producer with Maverick Productions in New York. I brought all those artists back to my favorite studio in Seattle.

When LPs started fading out of style in the late '70s, business slowed down. In 1980, I left Seattle and moved to Los Angeles. There, I worked at Mama Jo's Studio. The staff at Mama Jo's was Christian, and it had two labels. One label recorded Christian musicians, the other was a secular company that recorded such projects as Ambrosia and Donna Summer.

I, of course, was interested in the secular company.

"We have a Christian project coming up," someone in management told me. "The pay is good, and the musicians are excellent."

I decided to give it a try.

They went to the client and told him, "We have a man who isn't born again, but we're believing he will be. He's an excellent engineer. Will you try him?"

Kenneth Copeland and Doug Neece said, "Yes."

That was one of the most flawless sessions I've ever done in my life.

Doug Neece was Executive Director of the ministry back then, and he asked me to go back with him and have a look at the studio they'd built for Kenneth. It wasn't working.

I walked in, looked around and knew immediately what was wrong.

Although I was still employed full-time at Mama Jo's, the ministry began bringing me to Fort Worth to help with recording projects. Ironically, the first project I did was Kellie's album, *Refreshing Times*.

Kenneth and I hit it off, and he wanted me to work with him on his upcoming recordings. I helped with *Spirit Wind* and *Then Came the Morning*. Then he gave me a job on the TV truck and took me on the road.

Whenever I would finish a project and go back to Los Angeles, I'd miss the guys at the ministry. *They're great,* I remember thinking, *if only they knew what the real world was like.* I thought they had created a bubble in which they could exist, but it wasn't real.

I was soon to learn that it was *I* who didn't know reality.

As time passed, I was surprised to discover a lot of musicians I'd worked with previously were now in Kenneth's band. Mike Deasy, who had worked with Elvis, the Beach Boys and Bo Diddley, was one of them. I remember my shock at seeing him. *Mike—in Kenneth's band?*

I was in Fort Worth for a project one day when someone invited me to staff chapel. I agreed to go. It was a divine appointment.

I gave my heart to Jesus that day.

Afterward, Mike Deasy led me to a quiet room and I was filled with the Holy Spirit.

Today, that room is my office.

Although I enjoyed working with all the Copelands, there was one member of the family that particularly caught my attention.

Kellie.

I found myself wanting to know her better. And one day on a flight back from a meeting in Orlando, I got my chance. Kellie and I each had aisle seats across from one another.

I was very impressed by the things she said and I quickly decided I wanted to know more.

A few weeks later, we were both in Miami for a meeting and took a walk on the beach. We lived 1400 miles apart when we started dating. Yet, because our paths crossed so often, we saw one another every two weeks for the next six months.

By the end of that time, I knew what I wanted to do. I wanted to marry her. I waited to ask her until we were both among a group of friends and family on vacation. We'd traveled seven days and 300 miles through the Grand Canyon with Kenneth and Gloria. One night of that trip, out under the stars, I proposed.

Later, we all sat around a campfire and took turns giving our testimony. When my turn came, I was nervous. I stuck my foot in the dirt and kicked sand while I talked. Then, in a last rush, I said, "And I've asked Kellie to marry me."

Abruptly, I sat down.

After a momentary silence, Kenneth said, "Well, *what did she say?*"

She said, "Yes."

Even after we were married, I didn't plan on moving to Fort Worth any time soon. I owned my home in Los Angeles, and a good portion of my work was based there. It didn't take long to have second thoughts. The ministry started employing me almost 10 months out of the year, and as a married man, I knew Los Angeles wasn't the best place to raise a family.

I decided to put my house on the market just to see what would happen. I phoned the realtor who'd sold it to me.

"I'm not in the business anymore," she said, "but I'll send someone to you."

The man she sent was born again and Spirit filled.

He used to be a member of Vinita Copeland's Bible study.

My house sold in two days, for $10,000 more than I'd paid for it.

In February, 1986, God transplanted me to Fort Worth.

As manager of Kenneth's studio, the first thing I did was call Phil Driscoll,

Andrae Crouch and other Christian musicians I knew. "This is a great studio," I told them. "Come on out, and I'll give you two days free." None of them came.

Nothing I tried to book the studio worked.

Finally, one day I stood looking out the window of my office. "Lord," I prayed, "what am I doing here? After all the training I've been through, and everything I've learned, why did You bring me from Los Angeles out here to a cow pasture where nothing is happening? Am I going to dry up and blow away?"

You've been trying to bring artists here through the arm of the flesh, He said. *If you bring them, then it's your job to keep them. If I bring them, keeping the studio booked is My job.*

I repented, and rolled the care of the studio over onto the Lord.

Within two weeks, *He* had it booked, and it has stayed booked ever since. Today, we have a world-class recording studio. Musicians like Mylon Le Fevere, Phil Driscoll, Tim Miner, Donny McGuire and Reba Rambo are among those who travel to this cow pasture to record.

The Lord has blessed us with such an awesome team of people, that when I'm on the road as Kenneth's band leader, I know the studio will run smoothly.

In 1988, I was asked to head up the record labels and publishing company.

That's when I became Director of Music and producer of Kenneth's music.

Meanwhile, Kenneth found out about my deep-seated love of flying. I'd earned my pilot's license in 1982, and actually owned a small plane while I was managing the studio in Seattle. After my move to Los Angeles, I'd been too busy to pursue flying.

"I'd like to fly with you," Kenneth said.

We flew around together, and I told him I was working on my instrument rating. "Well," he said, "if you're going to fly with me, you're going to school."

I earned my instrument and multi-engine ratings in 11 days. The next thing I knew, I was in jet school.

Today, Kellie and I are richly blessed with four children.

My love of engineering is fulfilled in the studio.

I'm leader of one of God's greatest bands.

And if that weren't enough, I am a pilot for the ministry as well.

You might say that I'm living in the center of my dream.

If you won't give up, you can live in the center of *yours.*

W i n   K u t z

John and Marty
Copeland with their
daughter, Courtney

While I was growing up, all I ever wanted was a *normal* family. A family that wasn't any different than my friends' families. A family that didn't travel. I thoroughly disliked traveling. I remember complaining about it to my mother.

"Mother," I said, "I wish Daddy was a car salesman."

"A *car salesman?*" she asked, obviously surprised.

"Yeah, or anything *normal.*"

She sat down and explained to me about how many people Daddy was helping. I didn't care. We were different than everyone else. To a boy rapidly approaching his teens, being different was the worst thing that could happen.

Since this ministry has *always* been a family affair, I did my part like everyone else. I spent summers duplicating tapes, labeling tapes or cutting grass. Sometimes my parents took me with them to various meetings. After a while, I'd get bored and start checking out the auditorium.

More than once, I remember hearing Daddy introduce me and call me onstage. Unfortunately, I was usually in the catwalk overlooking the audience. He finally stopped introducing me.

By the time I reached my teenage years, I had an attitude. People were always asking me when *I* was going to start preaching. I wanted to be *me,* and not just Kenneth Copeland's son. Somehow, at that age, I couldn't see how I could be *both.*

I set out to prove to all my friends that I wasn't just a sissy preacher's kid. I proved my point by rebelling against God. I proved my point with alcohol, and with drugs. But no drug or alcohol could dim the fact that I *knew* what I was doing was wrong.

Mother and Dad were learning to walk by faith when I was a baby. It was such a lifestyle in our home, that I knew how to operate by faith before I even knew how to read or write.

I also saw miracles from the time I was old enough to remember. All the things my parents struggled to learn were just *common* to me. In fact, even *miracles* became commonplace to me.

To put it mildly, I *wasn't* an easy kid to deal with—and more often than not, my mother was the one who had to do the *dealing.* Of course, she was always very loving and patient, but I frequently tested her limits. I discovered that I could push her a long way before she'd have enough.

I'll never forget one night when I was a kid, she told me to go to bed. Then she told me again. I don't know how many chances she gave me, but I wasn't about to go to bed. There was a couch between us when she realized my intentions. I'd pushed her too far. In a flash of wisdom, I knew that a sofa wouldn't protect me from consequences. Sure enough, she jumped flat-footed right over it! But I was in bed before she reached me.

I used to think my mother was hard on me. Then I realized it was the *Lord*. He told her everything I did. She could be out of the country when I did something wrong, but the Holy Ghost would tell her exactly what I'd done. Pretty soon, the phone would ring.

"John…"

Being the oldest child in a large family, I think Mother grew up really fast.

Because of that, she's always been a hard worker, but she still loves adventure. She didn't just send us out to play. She played with us. When we were old enough to go out in the country and ride four-wheelers, she often rode one with us. She absolutely loves being outdoors. That's one of the things we have in common.

I noticed something about her back then. When she'd get in a tight spot, she didn't slow down to a crawl or stop to figure out what to do.

She'd give it gas.

I still tease her. "When in doubt—gas it!"

She often had to "put the pedal to the metal" when dealing with me! She poured on prayer and faith every time I was in trouble—and that was a good portion of the time!

Of course, Daddy was steady in faith for me too. But by the time I was 16, my relationship with him was rocky. About that time the Lord spoke to him about it. *John thinks you think he's a bad boy,* the Holy Spirit said.

"Lord, You know I don't think that about John," Dad answered.

You magnify his faults instead of his strengths.

Soon after that, Daddy called me aside to talk. "John," he said, "I want you to know that I love you. In fact, there is nothing you could ever do that would make me stop loving you. If you committed the worst crime in the world, I would love you and stand by you. I would never leave you.

"The Lord told me that I've magnified your faults, and that you think I think you're a bad boy. I don't, John. I think you are a son of God, and my brother in Christ.

"I want you to know that from this day forward, I will treat you like a man instead of a boy. However you choose to live your life is up to you. I'm going to be here for you and love you no matter what."

That took all the fun out of rebellion.

My behavior didn't change right away. In fact, outwardly, things looked worse. But something changed on the inside of me that day. Instead of finding ways to prove myself to my buddies, I started thinking about how Dad had *always* stood by me.

I'd been so busy trying to find an identity *different* than his, I hadn't appreciated our similarities.

After high school, I started my own welding business. As always, my parents stood by me. They treated me with the same pride and respect they would have given me if I'd been in worldwide ministry.

Welding suited me just fine. I loved being outdoors, and I enjoyed physical labor. From time to time, the ministry needed some welding done, and they hired me to do it. I enjoyed using my skills for the ministry.

After five years on my own, the ministry hired me full time to work with construction and maintenance. I liked the idea of being a part of what God was doing through the ministry at a place where I felt comfortable. My uncle, Doug Neece, was the Executive Director back then, and occasionally he'd sit down and talk to me about my future. Those talks made me uncomfortable. Sometimes he'd tell me to come into the office for a day or two just to learn the routine.

I dreaded those days. I didn't like being indoors. I didn't like wearing a suit.

Probably as much as Dad disliked having his face powdered for television.

Eventually, I was appointed Facilities Director. I supervised building maintenance, construction, telecommunications and our transportation department. Later, I was also given responsibility for security and aviation.

John and his dad have grown closer over the years because of Kenneth's unconditional love.

During those years, while God was growing the ministry, He was also growing in me. It was impossible to stay in the ministry atmosphere without having my heart and vision stretched. I knew that God had purpose for my life.

Somewhere along the way, I decided to fulfill that purpose regardless of the cost.

I decided to stop running from God's plan for my life.

In 1992, seven years after I went to work for the ministry, I was appointed International Director. By then, Marty and

I had a daughter, Courtney. Suddenly *I* was the father traveling all over the world, when the only place I wanted to be was home. I finally understood the price my father paid to obey God.

The next few years were hard on Marty and me. It seemed like I would be home for a week and gone again the next. At the same time, it was satisfying to know I was in God's will. It was satisfying to establish better communication with our international offices, and make sure we were all fulfilling the same goal. At home, I worked hard to get the local departments to think internationally whenever they did a project.

During that time, I was also given a large part of the responsibility for domestic meetings. No more exploring the catwalks for me. We had our equipment and crew flown into an area, set up for the meeting and afterward disassembled everything. So when I wasn't flying out of the country, I was flying to some city to set up for a meeting.

I was home even less.

By then, George Pearsons was Executive Director of Kenneth

John Copeland, future International Director of Kenneth Copeland Ministries.

Copeland Ministries. When George took over as pastor of Eagle Mountain International Church, he made me his Office Manager and began grooming me for the director position.

I've been Executive Director since 1995. When I first took over the job, I heard businessmen talking. "You have to have a one-year plan," they'd say. "And a five-year, 10-year, 20-year, and 30-year plan."

I can't seem to come up with a three-month plan, much less a one-year plan! I thought.

Finally, I went to talk to my parents.

"I feel like I'm falling short," I told them. "I know it's important to have a business plan, but I can't seem to make one we can stick with."

"I know exactly what you're talking about," Dad said. "It's OK to make a plan as long as you realize it can go out the window with one Word from God. The way we've had success is by taking a step at a time, but also stepping out in any direction that the Lord leads. Don't let a plan keep you from following God."

Dad dramatically demonstrated that principle after a convention in Australia in 1988. On the way home from that meeting, Dad said, "God says we're going on daily television."

That one word dramatically changed the course of this ministry.

Daily television wasn't in the plans.

That's the way I've tried to direct this ministry. We make plans and projections, but we will not be led by a plan. We're going to be led by the Lord.

These days, the Lord keeps telling me, *Get ready for increase.*

Based on that word, we're making plans. We're getting every department ready for increase. We're getting ready for a harvest.

Most days, I don't feel any more qualified for this position than Dad felt the first time he walked into an invalid room. If we left it up to feelings, we both would have bolted and never stopped running.

But this journey isn't about feelings, it's about faith.

It isn't about who I am, or who Kenneth Copeland is. It's about Who *God* is—in us.

Lord, keep me from living a *normal* life.

John Copeland

*L*ooking back, I can see the hand of God weaving my life together with the Copeland family and preparing me for a life in ministry, long before I ever dreamed of marrying John. From the fact that Kenneth led my dad to the Lord, to my wrestling with a weight problem, to my call to ministry, every step of the way, God was preparing me to marry John, and marry a ministry.

I wouldn't have it any other way.

When Kenneth was in his teens, he met and briefly worked for my dad. That would have been about 10 years before John or I were born. Several years later, my parents' best friends gave my mom some teaching and music tapes by Kenneth. My mom received the Baptism in the Holy Spirit.

By the time John and I met, I was 7 and he was 5. It wasn't exactly love at first sight. To me, he was just Kellie's little brother. Kellie and I were the same age, and we were good friends. Although we didn't see a lot of one another, there was a special bond between us that still exists today.

When I was in the third grade, we went to hear Kenneth preach. After the service, I was upset about something I thought no one knew about. When we all got in the car, Kenneth reached over and prayed for me. I was stunned.

I was just a little kid, but Kenneth cared about *my* feelings. And I knew God must care, too.

I grew up listening to eight-track tapes of Kenneth singing, as well as teaching tapes by Kenneth and Gloria.

I remember sharing with Kenneth and Gloria how, when I was 8 years old, Mom and I prayed for my perfect mate.

I wanted to marry a dark-haired, green-eyed cowboy, live on a lake, teach aerobics, be involved in ministry and write books.

God did really good!

Kenneth and Gloria figured out that they prayed for John's mate the same year.

When John and I were grown, our paths crossed again. He asked me out a few times. I said no each time. Having known John all my life, I had the strange idea that we didn't have anything in common. Even my dad started asking me, "Why don't you go out with John Copeland?"

When John told Gloria, "I'm not ever going to ask Marty for another date," she urged him, "John, just ask her one more time."

He did, and we were married in 1987.

I grew up in a family of 10. And we all helped in the family business. I learned first-hand the responsibility, commitment and sacrifice it takes to work with family. Most importantly, I learned to honor those in authority.

When I married John, I understood right away what it meant to pitch in and help in any way I could.

Over the years, I've worked in the music department, ministry correspondence, and been a member of the intercessory prayer team praying over Partners' letters. Today, I'm a personal trainer, and I minister in the area of health and fitness

through teaching Bible seminars and through my video, *Arise and Walk,* and workout cassette, *Walkin' Free.* I also counsel KCM staff members in regard to their nutrition and exercise.

By far the greatest joy of my life is being John's wife and a mother to our daughter, Courtney.

But the two most impacting experiences I've had have been assisting Gloria with Healing School, and helping put together Kenneth's Bible notes for the *Kenneth Copeland Reference Edition* Bible.

Because of my own call to minister to people in the area of health and fitness, I have been especially drawn to the ministry of Healing School. To see people made whole and well is important to me. I appreciate the opportunity to meet people and prepare them to release their faith as Gloria lays hands on them. With each Healing School, I learn more from Gloria about God and more from God about people.

My responsibility in assisting with Kenneth's study Bible was to assemble six to eight years of his sermon outlines for publication.

As I sat on the floor of John's and my home, with stacks of Kenneth's private study notes around me, I read revelations that were as fresh as the moment the Holy Spirit shared them with Kenneth.

Often John came home to find me weeping over the pages.

I cried because of the depth of this man's love for God.

I cried because of the magnitude of faith it took to do what Kenneth and Gloria were called to do.

I cried because of the privilege given me to look deep into the heart of a man—and the joy of seeing nothing but unselfishness, integrity and faith, the likes of which I'd never seen.

There was one page, in particular, that I will never forget. The page was blank except for these words:

It's better to give the wrong man a break, than to break the wrong man.

I didn't just weep because I discovered new things about Kenneth Copeland.

I wept because I discovered new things about God.

M a r t y   C o p e l a n d

Kenneth and grand-
daughter Courtney

Terri Copeland Pearsons is still comfortable with a microphone in hand as she pastors Eagle Mountain International Church with her husband, George.

Future Commander Kellie

Chief Executive Officer of Kenneth Copeland Ministries, John Copeland

Terri, John and Kellie,1971

"My Father's Work," a childhood drawing by John Copeland.

The family celebrates Kenneth's 60th birthday. Left to right: John, Kellie, Gloria, Kenneth and Terri.

Gloria and her mother, Mary Neece

Big sister Gloria with her brothers and sister in 1958 (left to right):
Doug, Richard, Tommy, Jan and Gloria.

Gloria's father, Wallace Neece, holding his granddaughter, Kellie
Copeland, 1964.

Celebrating Kenneth's 60th Birthday

Kenneth with his
Aunt Mackie

Gloria's brothers and sisters.
(Left to right): Doug, Richard,
Jan, Missy and Tommy.

Four generations...Mary Neece,
Kellie Copeland Kutz, her daughter,
Rachel and Gloria Copeland.

…And the greatest revival of all shall be in the prisons of the land. Great ministers of the gospel shall come out of prisons all over this nation. All over this world.

**Prophecy delivered by Kenneth Copeland
at Eagle Mountain International Church,
Fort Worth, Texas, on December 25, 1994**

*…I don't know who you are, or where you are in this building, but there's somebody in this building, there's someone in your family who was sentenced to the penitentiary today. And the Lord wanted me to tell you, Don't worry and wring your hands in concern, because I will watch over him. And I will be with him. And I will deliver him, and I will deliver him in better shape than when he left…
Don't cry over that anymore,
I know it's hard to take, but don't cry over it anymore. This is not the end. This is the beginning.*

**Prophecy delivered by Kenneth Copeland
at Washington, D.C. Victory Campaign,
February 3, 1994**

CHAPTER 8

Reaching Out

I was hungry and you gave Me food; I was thirsty and you gave Me drink; I was a

stranger and you took Me in; I was naked and you clothed Me; I was sick and you

visited Me; I was in prison and you came to Me. MATTHEW 25:35-36

 lmost from the day God called me into this ministry, I've had a desire to minister to prisoners. I knew that if the Church would take the Word of God behind the iron bars, those inmates would be set free—really free—by the truth of Jesus Christ. The worst prison in the world isn't any penal system. It's the prison of darkness that comes from being bound by Satan's lies.

In 1994, close to 400 inmates from Texas prisons signed petitions asking Gloria and me to come minister to them. Praise God, we went! On the Friday and Saturday after Thanksgiving, we ministered to the male inmates at Coffield. The prison allowed Mike Barber to erect his tent, and hundreds of spiritually hungry inmates gathered to hear about God. Between services, 40 men from Eagle Mountain International Church joined 100 other volunteers to minister from cell to cell under the leadership of Mike Barber Ministries.

In September of that same year, Gloria toured four women's facilities and ministered to the inmates and officers. "Your body may be in prison," she said, "but your spirit doesn't need to be there. You can be in prison, but prison doesn't have to be in you."

(Facing page)
Hundreds of inmates
heard the life-changing
message of the gospel
during the 1994 tent
meeting.

Ministering to four women on death row, she shared Hebrews 2:14, declaring that believers have done all the dying they're going to do. She encouraged them to continue to claim their covenant privileges, including long life. She also asked them to use their time in prison to pray for the Church—especially that the working of miracles, gifts of healing and the gift of faith be manifested in the closing of these last days.

In 1995, we partnered with Mike Barber Ministries, and we began working with Texas officials on the installation of satellite systems in 87 Texas prisons. That was the first year we broadcast our motorcycle rally into Texas prisons, as well as prisons in Arkansas and Oklahoma. We also began broadcasting a Christmas program into the prisons each year. The response to all the broadcasts has been awesome.

Every time we minister in a prison, or send them a broadcast through satellite, our personal correspondence with inmates soars. Back in 1993, we received 70 to 100 letters a day from inmates—totaling no more than 36,500 for the year. In 1995, after broadcasting the motorcycle rally and Christmas program by satellite, our correspondence leapt to an amazing *193,787 letters!* As revival began shaking the prisons in 1996, the effects brought an unparalleled 290,047 letters from inmates.

These prisoners are hungry for the Word of God. Many, many times, they tell us that the Word-based teaching and materials they receive from KCM have made a great impact on their lives. We are happy to be able to offer them tapes, videos and teaching materials, books, Bibles and our devotional book, *From Faith to Faith.* We watched in awe as *Faith to Faith* became KCM's most requested book in prison systems across this nation. Every new prisoner admitted to Tucker Prison in Arkansas is given a *Faith to Faith.* This is just further evidence that the Word of God changes lives *everywhere.*

At two state prisons, our materials have become the curriculum in a Bible school that disciples ministers among the inmates and trains pastors to pastor inmates.

Recently, the Lord has opened our eyes to the needs of a whole new population of people, hungry for God in this weary world. They are criminal youth between the ages of 10 and 16. For all those, regardless of age, who've been tried and found guilty in men's courts, there is no better news than Jesus. Because He suffered the Cross, God's final verdict resounds throughout eternity.

"Not guilty!"

Kenneth

Gloria's Favorite Letter

Gloria:

Yo, a note from behind the bars to say hay. Thank you and your ole man. Saved me from hanging in hell, truely a unpayable debt.

About two years ago my ole lady left me and left me kicking with a tude. So me and my bros started pushen the crank and Jhonie law was on my tail. It didn't take long and I was slambed in the stir and my bros ran like dogs with all my goods, and my lady friend kicked me to the curb.

Hay, I was lost and way out there too, and I didn't like where I was. I wanted to hang it up. I quit eating, started fights in hopes I'd git killed, but the spirit came to me and lined me out. I found you and Ken on the tube and between you, Ken and the gost, the three of you pulled me through it (Hay, I don't mean to space the Boss, he put it together). Oh, ya, Jesus too. Whoo, there was a hole wor party out to save my Junkie butt, but hay I thought I was abanded and there ya all were. I'll never say thank you enuf not to you and Ken.

I've just been kicken in my crib and reading the book. Just me, the Boss and the brother; we got a good thing. I haven't been in a fight or put nothing in my arm. I even give up the ciggarette.

I was on the max block, but I asked the brother to help me out and when the next day I got put to Medium I asked for some bucks and within a week my Mouther flew me a kite with a yard in it. I hadn't heard from her in over five years. She just happened to read about my bust in the news rag.

One day I was talken to the Boss and I said, "You don't want no biker trash man. I ain't no good a-tall to ya." Well, I turned on your flick and there you were on stage talking to a hole pasture full of us that spun me. We have been along ways since then. There is this home boy on this block that looks just like I did only one year ago, but I was spooked about throwen out a line for fear that my thinking wasn't right. I found your rag walking in the spirit. Yo, I had the gost tell me everything you said like I read the book long ago, but I know I hadn't.

Well, I talked to some bros about the Boss and hay, they hang with him to (it wasn't quite as easy as it sounded, but you git my drift, I'm sure).

So, thanks once more. You two are good in my book and can hang with me any time. I relly love you guys. There is alot I'd like to share, but don't have enuf sit down so I bet I'll see ya on the high way.

Thanks.

Love
K.C. S.

Prison Letters

TEXAS DEPARTMENT OF
CRIMINAL JUSTICE

Dear Brother,

Several days ago we received a "Loving Care Package" from Kenneth Copeland Ministries, and I want you to know that hearts were touched, mine included. I had a man who had been asking for weeks for a large print Bible. As you know, the prison system does not furnish things like this. Just about all the gifts we receive go to buying indigent supplies for men who get no money from home. When the Bibles came, I called a man who desperately needed a Bible he could read. When he saw the Bible Kenneth Copeland Ministries had provided, we both began to weep.

Volunteer Chaplain
Huntsville, Texas

CORRECTIONS CORPORATIONS
OF AMERICA

Dearest Kenneth and Gloria;

…The men have prayed over and over that God would send you here to minister. I have never seen so much childish expectation on the faces of so many grown men in my life. It helps me understand what Jesus meant when He spoke of coming to God as a little child.

A. H.

TEXAS DEPARTMENT OF
CRIMINAL JUSTICE

Dear Kenneth Copeland,

On behalf of the residents here at E. Glossbrenner Unit, I want to thank you for your program aired December 21, 1995. Two hundred and thirty-seven of our residents viewed the program. Many of them made commitments to the Lord, and many more were ministered to by the praise and worship music, and by the powerful Word of God preached by you and Mike Barber.

J. T., Chaplain

Prison Letters

NEW RIVER CORRECTIONAL INSTITUTION

Dear Friends in Christ:

   …I especially want to thank you for the July issue of the *Believer's Voice of Victory* magazine. …As I read Brother and Sister Copeland's articles, the anointing of the Holy Spirit upon them was incredible. I read, reread, studied, and prayed over them. Then, on July 16, I told the inmates in the chapel service that they needed to read and study those messages…

Senior Chaplain

STATE OF CONNECTICUT DEPARTMENT OF CORRECTIONS

Dear KCM,

   …The testimonies I hear about your excellent teaching material is inspiring. Each time I hand the men one of your daily devotional books they shine…

Reverend C.

Ministering to the prisoners (left to right): Mike and Deanne Barber, Jesse and Cathy Duplantis, Gloria and Kenneth Copeland.

Dear K.C. Ministries;

I am an inmate at the Racine Correctional Institution. I became a Christian 12 years ago, and have been an inmate for 13 years. In this time I have grown so much that my family doesn't recognize me anymore. But during this time I also fell into the old trap taught by religion. I believed that God does certain things for certain people. I believed that God wouldn't even mess with our physical world or our physical needs, desires, and situations. Oh, He would concern Himself in these things for certain people, but not for the everyday, ordinary Christian.

Then I got some of the tapes and reading material that your ministry puts out. The wall I had built around me for my protection was blasted away. I found out that this wall was the very thing that was restricting God from working in my life. The Holy Spirit opened my eyes, my ears, my understanding, and my faith.

Two weeks ago I broke out in praise and I haven't stopped since. One day this week I broke out in a praise session, and

Between services, volunteers ministered from cell to cell.

before I knew it, for the first time in my life, I found myself speaking in tongues. A habit I've had as long as I can remember just fell away from me. The desire for television has passed away—all I want to do is hear the Word of God, speak the Word of God, and stand on the Word of God…

Name Withheld

Dear Mr. Copeland:

It's the first day of a brand new month and I couldn't help but reminisce on where I was just last year at this time. In 1988 I was incarcerated for embezzlement and I was living for the devil. Almost seven years later, I was finally led to the Lord and I have you and your wife to thank for that. I believe that God spoke to me through a daydream and showed me what could happen in my life if I turned things around. The next day I spoke with an officer, who was a Christian, and she shared with me a little about Jesus and His mercy. However, it wasn't until a fellow inmate had ordered a *Faith to Faith* book, and you sent her two, that I was actually saved. She asked me if I wanted to read the extra copy, and I agreed for lack of anything better to do. I had never read the Bible, and grew up in a broken family without church or faith. I can remember being taught to say, "Now I lay me down to sleep…" but that was the extent of my prayers. Now, all of a sudden, I was reading a book that touched my heart and I asked Jesus to come into my life. From that moment, everything changed…

I was determined to do one thing in my life that was right—believe in God and His Word….

Today, I am out of prison and married to the man I loved years ago. He has started a church, and teaches a Rhema Bible study class on Monday nights. On Tuesday nights, I go to the nursing home ministry. We have church on Wednesday, and praise and worship practice on Thursday. Then church on Sunday. For someone who never went to church before, you can't keep me out now!

…Less than nine months ago I was living in a dorm with 75 other women. Now, I am reunited with my daughter whom I home school all day to make up for the time I lost with her. I live in a "mansion" in Georgia, with a loving husband, beautiful daughter, a fabulous church, a job I love, and a baby boy on the way.

Who can doubt that God is real?

K.

*I*n 1990, a representative of the Full Gospel Motorcycle Association International asked me if they could have a motorcycle rally here on the grounds of Eagle Mountain. Gloria and I liked the idea so much, we invited them to come. Jerry Savelle, Jesse Duplantis, Gloria and I participated in the rally, which drew several hundred bikers.

The following year, we became more involved with the Full Gospel Motorcycle Association International as they hosted the FGMAI "Wings of Freedom" Rally here at Eagle Mountain. Over 2300 people showed up!

Beginning in 1992, Kenneth Copeland Ministries became the sole sponsor of the rally, and it was officially named the Eagle Mountain Motorcycle Rally. We ran an ad in the *Believer's Voice of Victory* magazine, not knowing how many bikers would respond. More than 4,000 people from 45 states and six nations came together for the weekend of ministry, fellowship and fun. Gloria and I, Jerry and Jesse preached the Word. Mac Gober and Ben Priest of the Tribe of Judah also joined us in ministering to the people, and hundreds gave their hearts to the Lord.

By 1994, the number attending the rally had grown to nearly 13,000! God continued to add men and women of God to help reach them.

About 15,000 people converged at Eagle Mountain for the 1995 Motorcycle Rally. As a result of Mike Barber's involvement and the open doors with prisons, the evening services were broadcast live by satellite to 87 of the 104 state prisons in Texas. This gave more than 150,000 men and women the opportunity to hear the Word of God. Prisons in at least 15 other states were also able to receive the satellite signal. One local prison chaplain showed a videotape of the rally to 100 inmates. When Mac Gober gave an invitation to receive Jesus, every man stood up.

Only the Lord knows how many souls were saved during that rally. But we do know that after the Sunday service here at Eagle Mountain, 1106 people waded into Eagle Mountain Lake to be baptized.

In 1996, registration for the rally totaled 10,037, but many thousands more attended the services. According to the Tarrant County Sheriff's Department, which controlled the bumper-to-bumper traffic, over 40,000 people were counted in attendance during the course of the weekend.

Riding two by two on the "pack ride" around Fort Worth, the line of motorcycles stretched over the horizon. Campsites dotted the terrain with thousands of tents and numerous recreational vehicles. In this extraordinary setting, it was possible to bring the gospel to people who might never attend a church.

John G. Lake, that powerful man of God who took Africa by storm, called the truth of Jesus Christ "a strong man's gospel." The strong man's gospel he talked about draws thousands of bikers to Eagle Mountain each year. These strong men and women of God are not reserved or quiet about their faith. When the rally ends, armed with a strong gospel, they ride away to prisons, halfway houses and outlaw biker gangs. They remember what many people have forgotten.

Jesus never sent the world to church. He sent the Church to the world.

Kenneth

Thousands fill the KCM grounds during the 1993 Eagle Mountain Motorcycle Rally.

Good Friends and Fun

A merry heart doeth good like a medicine... PROVERBS 17:22

The Lord has blessed me with many good friends over the years, but the *best* friends I have are the people who have partnered with me in this ministry. Those are the people I write letters to every month.

I learned the importance of letter writing from my spiritual father, Oral Roberts. Years ago, he called me aside and said, "I want to see you for the next several days."

The first day I went to his house, he sat at his desk. I sat across from him. We'd been talking for a few minutes when he held up his Bible.

"What is this?" he asked.

"That's the Word of God."

"What is this?" he asked again.

Obviously, I hadn't given him the answer he wanted.

"Well," I said, "it's the Old Covenant and the New Covenant."

"What *is* this?" he asked a third time.

"It's the Bible."

Wham! He threw that Bible and hit me in the stomach with it.

"Those are *letters!*" he said. "And they're just as anointed today as they were the day they were written!"

Letters!

I'd seen that look on his face before.

(Facing page)
Kenneth reading
letters from his
Partners.

The anointing was all over him.

"I'm going to ask you to make one of the most serious commitments you've ever made in your life," he explained. "I want you to commit to God that every 30 days for the rest of your life you will pray in the Holy Ghost until *you* have something anointed to write to your Partners, just the way Paul wrote to his."

I looked at that Bible as though I was seeing it for the first time. Those letters were born in intercession! I could almost hear Paul's voice, "I bow my knees before my heavenly Father, calling you to remembrance. Though I am absent in the body, I am present in the spirit, beholding your order."

"How do I write letters like that?" I asked God later as I thought about what Brother Roberts had said to me.

Read one until you learn how, He answered.

So that's what I did. I started studying one of the most awesome letters a man of God ever wrote to his ministry partners— the book of Philippians.

From that time until now, I've written a letter every month to my friends who are in partnership with me. They aren't money-raising letters. I don't write them for that reason. *God* is my source, and *He* meets all my needs. I write the letters because I want to bless my Partners. Since they are partakers of my grace (Philippians 1:7), I want to share with them the revelations God has given me.

I agonize over those letters. I pray, and pray, and pray, and pray. Then I go back to prayer until I hear what's on God's heart. Sometimes it comes to me in the middle of the night. But one thing's for sure. I wait until I hear from heaven. I *don't* just sit down and put something on paper.

As a result, those letters have changed lives—my Partners' and *mine.* Thanks to God, and to the Holy Spirit working through the Apostle Paul and Brother Roberts, we have all been blessed!

Kenneth

Oral and Evelyn Roberts with Kenneth

I've always known that it took a lot of people to pray through what God has done in our lives and ministry. Ken and I not only trust that people are praying, we *experience* the effect of those prayers. Every now and then, the Lord demonstrates His faithfulness where prayer is concerned in a fresh, new way.

He did it again recently with this precious letter.

Vinita must have given that picture of Ken to Beulah more than 40 years ago! Yet, this dear saint has treasured not only the photograph, but her prayer commitment as well.

Who knows the victories we've won because of unknown souls like Beulah Siegle.

And *you*.

G l o r i a

Houston, Texas
March 8, 1997

Dear Kenneth and Gloria,

This is a letter that I have procrastinated over for some time. The Lord has been dealing with me for some time to write you.

Where do I begin—Ken, I knew your mother. We met… in the 1950s in Ardmore, Oklahoma, on the lake where the camps were held spring and fall. We were friends, and I was in her home one time. We did not keep in as close touch as I wish we had as time moved on. As is well-known, she was one of the greatest women of prayer I have ever known. She gave me a snapshot of you. Maybe you were a teenager, I don't remember.

I gave her a picture of my only child, a daughter, and we agreed to pray each for the other. You both are near the same age…

I have just had a birthday January 9, 1997. I am 90 years old…I spend much time in prayer and study, and your preaching and ministry have meant life to me…

How good the dear Lord is…. May He bless you according to all the joy and hope you have and are to hundreds of thousands. That will sure be a lot of blessings.

With you in His kingdom
Lovingly,
Beulah Siegle

erry Savelle started working with me when he wasn't much more than a skinny kid. He didn't have but one suit of clothes to wear to our meetings. But he was full of the fire of God. In the early days, when he traveled with me and handled the tapes, sound, transportation and everything else for our meetings, Jerry used to go out on the beach and win more people than we did in the meeting that evening! We were in Omaha, Nebraska, one time on a Sunday morning. Jerry had gone downtown to find someone. There were people everywhere, most of them going to church.

Right in the middle of the crowd, a guy had a grand mal seizure. He was flipping and flopping all over the sidewalk, and bounced right out in the street.

Jerry didn't look right or left. He didn't stop to ask anyone's permission.

He walked right through that crowd, grabbed the man by the head and said, "Come out of him, in the Name of Jesus!"

I want you to know people got away from him in a hurry. They gave him room to operate. He cast the devil out of that old boy, and his eyes rolled back around right. Someone called an ambulance, but Jerry had led the man to the Lord before it arrived.

Jerry helped load the man in the ambulance. When it drove away, the guy was looking out the back window saying, "Jesus…Jesus…Jesus…Jesus."

Jerry Savelle will turn any vacation into a pulpit.

If there's *air,* he's got a place to preach.

What do you think would happen if every believer stepped outside every morning and saw the world as their pulpit?

We'd win the world.

Kenneth

I didn't want any part of God in 1969, when Kenneth Copeland came to my hometown of Shreveport, Louisiana. Until then, I'd been fairly successful in eluding

Him. I hadn't allowed Jesus to be the Lord of my life for one good reason—I *knew* there was a call on my life to preach.

I didn't want to preach.

It seemed like the harder I pedaled to get *away* from God, the harder my wife prayed. Carolyn was born again, filled with the Holy Ghost, and serving God with all of her heart. She refused to let our lives go any direction but God's direction. She and her parents were active in church, but I only went on occasion.

Every time a preacher came to town to fill the pulpit, the pastor asked Carolyn's parents to let him stay at their house. The only problem with that was we lived *next door.*

It seemed like I'd been drug over to meet every minister who'd come to town. You can imagine my delight when Carolyn insisted that I meet Kenneth Copeland. She finally got me over there, and I cooled my heels in the den while he was shut up in the bedroom praying.

Finally, I'd had enough, and I turned to leave.

Just then, the bedroom door opened and he came out.

"Brother Copeland," my father-in-law said, "I'd like for you to meet my son-in-law, Jerry Savelle."

Kenneth and a young Jerry Savelle (right).

Brother Copeland waved at me and walked on into the kitchen to get a glass of water.

That's it! I thought, *I'm out of here.*

I'd almost reached the door when Brother Copeland said, "Wait a minute!" He pointed his finger at me. "God's going to prosper you."

Then he disappeared again.

I was furious.

Carolyn's been talking to him about my business! I fumed. I figured the only way he could have known I was going to prosper was if someone told him I owned my own business.

Carolyn begged me every night to go hear him preach, but I didn't want any part of it. She just about wore me out. Finally, to keep her quiet, I agreed to go to the last meeting.

"We'll sit on the back row closest to the exit," I bargained. "As soon as he starts telling those tear-jerking stories and begging for money, I'm leaving. You'll have to get home the best way you can."

"That's a deal!" she agreed.

He never did tell any tear-jerking stories, and he never begged for money. I walked away from church that night stunned.

"I've never heard the gospel like that before!" I told Carolyn.

Suddenly, God seemed real. Jesus no longer seemed in the same category as Santa Claus and the Easter bunny. The Bible no longer seemed like a storybook or a history lesson.

In one service, it all came alive to me.

I didn't run to the altar and surrender my life to God. I was too proud for that. But the next day, I went to my paint and body shop under deep conviction. I sent my employees home, grabbed the Bible that Carolyn had put on my desk and blew off the dust. I walked into the restroom, sat on the floor and cried all day.

Finally, at 3 in the morning on February 11, 1969, I lifted both hands and said, "Jesus, I can't run anymore. If there's anything left in me that You can possibly use, here it is. Take a good look, because I'm a failure. I'm only 22 years old, and I'm already a failure."

I'll never forget the words He spoke to me.

Don't worry about it, son. I'm a Master at making champions out of failures.

Have you ever felt like a failure?

You need to meet Jesus.

He can make a champion out of you.

Jerry Savelle

The week after Brother Copeland left Shreveport, a friend of Carolyn's dropped by the house with seven reel-to-reel tapes and a tape player. "God told me to bring you all of Brother Copeland's tapes from the meeting," she said, "and you're to listen to them."

I didn't listen to them immediately, but soon after surrendering my life to the Lord and to the ministry, I listened to the first one. That's when the Lord told me, *I want you to shut your business down and spend the next three months listening to those tapes no less than eight hours a day.*

I shut my business down, moved into my guest bedroom and set it up as my study room. Those seven tapes had a message on each side, and I listened to them over and over for three months.

I had so many questions, but when I'd ask some Christians, they would say things like, "Now, you've got to be careful of this faith stuff. Be careful of that Kenneth Copeland. He's an extremist."

I had 9,000 questions and no one to ask.

I'd had a particularly tough time believing God for finances. In the natural, I had no income because I had shut down my business, and I was sitting in that bedroom studying the Word. It was tough believing that my needs would be met.

At the end of those three months, Brother Copeland came back to town. I was sitting in the audience when he came out on the platform. He hadn't been sitting there too long before he motioned for me to come to him.

I walked up to the platform, and he took me into the choir room.

"The Lord just spoke to me," he said. "God says that you have some questions, and you've been wanting to talk to me about them."

"Yes," I agreed, "I've got a lot of questions. I'm listening to your tapes. I've learned how to believe God for healing. But I can't seem to figure out how to get God to bless me financially."

"Jerry," he said, "your problem is your big mouth. You need to learn the vocabulary of silence." Then, he turned around and walked away!

I went back to my seat, and the more I thought about him telling me my problem was my big mouth, the madder I got.

I'm probably the only guy in this whole church who believes anything you say, I fumed. *How dare you say my problem is my big mouth? I need a revelation from God!*

I was so *mad.* When I got home that night, I walked past the bedroom where I had been listening to all those tapes. I'd been listening to them for three months! All I did was ask the man a simple question, and he *insulted* me!

I grabbed the reel-to-reel tape that was on the tape player, and I walked outside. *I don't have to listen to this!*

I stepped out into the middle of the street and threw that tape as hard as I could. Then I stood there and watched it unwind as the reel rolled down the street.

It felt so good, I decided to roll them *all* down the street.

I ran back inside to get another one, and the Spirit of God spoke to me.

What are you doing?

"I'm getting rid of these tapes!" I said. "This stuff doesn't work!"

You're rolling the answer to your problem down the street.

"I asked the man a simple question, and he insulted me! All I wanted to know was how to believe You for finances."

He told you the right answer.

"He said the problem was my big mouth!"

That's right.

Then suddenly, God gave me supernatural recall of everything I'd been saying for the last three months.

One moment I'd confess, "My God meets all my needs!"

But under pressure I would say, "Dear God, I'm going broke!"

When the Lord gave me that instant replay of everything I'd been saying, I realized that what Brother Copeland said was true. I was negating everything I'd said that was positive with something negative. My financial problem was my own big mouth.

Suddenly it hit me. *The answer to my problem is rolling down the street!*

I ran outside and chased that tape down the street.

I brushed off the dirt and gravel, and carefully wound it back on the reel. Today, I still have all those tapes, and I still listen to them. I'm still grateful that Brother Copeland was willing to tell me the truth. That truth has forever changed me...and my big mouth.

A few months later, we found out that Brother Copeland was going to be preaching at Grace Temple in Fort Worth, Texas. We just knew that we were supposed to be in that meeting.

My old car was absolutely worn out with over 100,000 miles on it. But we were desperate to hear the Word, so we believed God for the gas money and believed that the old car would make the trip.

We arrived in time for the first evening meeting, and we felt as though we had just left "Egypt" and we were now in the "Promised Land."

After the service, because we had no extra money for a hotel, Carolyn and our two daughters and myself slept in the car in the parking lot at the church. But you know, we really didn't mind because we knew that what we were hearing was going to change our lives forever.

Well, over 25 years have come and gone and we haven't had to sleep in the parking lot since, nor have we had to be concerned about our car. The messages that Brother Copeland preached brought us from poverty to prosperity, from sickness to health and from failure to success.

The Savelles will forever be grateful to the Copelands for their faithfulness to preach the uncompromising Word of Faith.

Jerry Savelle

Jerry and Carolyn
Savelle

After I rescued my tapes from the street and got over being offended, I went back and attended the rest of the meetings Brother Copeland was preaching in Shreveport. I'm so thankful to God that I did.

During one of those meetings, Brother Copeland called me out of the audience and had me stand up.

"God just showed me that you and I will become a team," he prophesied. "And it's your responsibility to believe God for the perfect timing."

Me…a team with Brother Copeland?

I was so overwhelmed, I could hardly stand. *No wonder the devil wanted me offended.*

I didn't know one other person in my life, at that point, who knew God like Kenneth Copeland did. And he had just publicly invited me to be a part of his life and ministry.

Nine months passed without any contact between us. I didn't even know if Kenneth Copeland remembered me. In 1970, I was preaching at a youth meeting in Oklahoma City, and Brother Copeland was preaching in California.

During that meeting, he called my house and spoke to Carolyn.

"Tell Jerry that I'm going to be in Jacksonville, Florida, next week," he said. "Ask him to meet me there."

When I got in from Oklahoma City, we packed the car, loaded our girls and headed to Florida. I worked with him in that meeting, and afterward, he asked, "Jerry, when are you moving to Fort Worth?"

I didn't have to think about it.

"Next week," I said.

We drove back to Shreveport, packed everything and moved to Fort Worth, Texas.

The Lord told me to watch Brother Copeland like a hawk, and I would learn three things. First, He said I would learn how to preach with authority. Second, He said that I would learn to pray for the sick. Third, He said that I would learn how to tap into the wisdom of God.

It's been 28 years since the Lord spoke those words to me.

During those years, I've learned to preach with authority, pray for the sick and tap into the wisdom of God.

But that list wasn't exhaustive.

The Lord has taught me many other things through the years of being teamed with Brother Copeland. I've learned about giving, for example. During all those years, I've never met *anyone* who gives like Kenneth and Gloria. They truly live to give.

That spirit of giving that is on them has transformed my life, and the lives of those in my family. We too have discovered that a life of giving is the best kind of life there is!

Jerry Savelle

In 1969, the Lord told Kenneth that he and Jerry would become a team. Today they are still going strong, ministering the uncompromised Word of God.

Years ago, I went to Brother Copeland for advice. As usual, the place the devil was beating me was in the area of finances. I'll never forget what Brother Copeland said to me.

"Jerry, the shadow of a dog never bit anyone."

Then he walked away!

I couldn't *believe* that's all he was going to say. The shadow of a dog never bit anyone?

That's the craziest thing I've ever heard, I thought. *The man must be working too hard. His mind is slipping. He needs rest. That's the revelation I've been waiting to hear? Thank you, Brother Copeland, my problems are solved!*

Yet, those words just kept coming back to me. *The shadow of a dog never bit anyone.* Then I remembered that Psalm 23:4 doesn't say that we will walk through the *valley* of death. It says we'll walk through the *valley of the shadow* of death.

"Lord," I finally asked, "what does shadow mean?"

God directed me to the dictionary. The definition of shadow is, "a definite area of shade cast upon a surface by a body *intercepting the light rays.*"

As soon as I read that definition, I understood the devil's tactics. He wanted to intercept the light coming from God's Word, and cast a dark image on my thoughts so I would be controlled by fear.

When Brother Copeland said, "The shadow of a dog never bit anyone," he was saying, "Jerry, you're dealing with shadows. The devil is trying to convince you that your financial needs will never be met. It's a smoke screen—nothing but a shadow. Dogs bite, but their shadows never do."

I want to encourage you the way Brother Copeland encouraged me.

You're not in this alone. Jesus is by your side.

You may have been told, "There's not enough money!"

That's a shadow.

"You'll never be healed of that disease!"

That's a shadow.

"Your kids will never get off drugs!"

That's a shadow.

The next time something seems to be intercepting the Light of God's Word in your life, just remember. *The shadow of a dog never bit anyone!*

Jerry Savelle

I'll never forget a morning service in Springfield, Missouri, where Brother Copeland was preaching. It was 1972, and I hadn't been working with him for more than a couple of years.

I remember that he was teaching about the reality of righteousness, when a woman in the back of the room began waving her arm at him.

"Just a minute," he said to her, "I need to finish this point."

The woman just wouldn't wait. She interrupted him saying, "This can't wait. I have a word from God."

Finally, she created such a distraction that Brother Copeland stopped his sermon. "I guess I'm going to have to let you talk," he said, "since you're going to interrupt me anyway."

She started out OK, but after a few sentences, it was clear that this woman was influenced by an evil spirit. While she was talking, she stepped out into the aisle and started swinging her arms up and down.

"I see You, Jesus!" she called, looking up above Brother Copeland's head. "You told me You would come down here today and pick me up and fly away!"

Then, she started flapping her arms like a bird in flight.

Every person in the room looked at him to see what he would do about her—including me. It only took a few seconds to find out.

"Jerry!" he ordered, "get that woman out of here! Get her delivered, and don't leave her until she's free!"

I stood rooted to the floor.

Me? He wants me *to get this woman delivered? I thought* he *was the faith man!*

"Did you hear me?" he barked. "I said for you to get her *out of here!* Get her *delivered,* and don't leave her until she's *free!*"

I forced myself to move toward her. When I got close enough, I reached for her hand, and she jerked it away.

I grabbed her hand again, and she jerked it away.

How am I supposed to get her out of here?

Finally, I grabbed her and pulled her out by force.

At the back of the building, I opened the door on the right.

It was a parking lot filled with people.

I opened the door on the left.

It was a kitchen filled with people.

I opened the door in the very back.

A cloak closet! Perfect!

I pulled her inside and slammed the door.

Where's the light switch?

I fumbled in the dark for the light switch while she flapped her wings.

Then she slugged me.

I pulled myself up and fought her off until I finally found the switch.

She was coming after me again.

"God, what am I supposed to do?"

Use the Name!

"Come out of her in the Name of Jesus!"

The Name of Jesus seemed to have a calming effect, so I prayed harder and louder. Finally, I was shouting, **"I bind you in the Name of Jesus! Now loose her and set her free!"**

Every person in a two mile radius heard me.

Then I prayed in tongues.

I struggled with that woman, wrestled with her, prayed for her and finally….I got her delivered, born again and filled with the Holy Spirit.

Then, I opened the door to the cloakroom.

Everyone was gone!

They had finished the service, and gone off and left me with that woman!

I turned and looked at her. She was praying in tongues. The glory of God was on her face.

I decided that it didn't matter so much that they left *me*.

What really counted was that the devil left *her*.

Jerry Savelle

At a Believers'
Convention, Jerry
demonstrates how
to dress for battle
and take an aggres-
sive stand against
the enemy.

I'll never forget my first motorcycle trip with Kenneth and Gloria. I was used to riding a smaller Harley, but I'd just bought a *big* bike. Cathy and I had a trailer hooked onto the back of the thing. We were equipped and ready to travel.

Everything was going smoothly until we pulled over onto the side of the road. I slowed down on the shoulder and leaned over so I could put my foot down. When I did, the shoulder gave way and we started falling.

"Bail out, Mama!" I shouted at Cathy as 900 pounds of metal started rolling over on us. We didn't take a vote on what to do next. We *jumped!*

We went flying off that motorcycle and rolled halfway down the embankment before we came to a stop. I looked up to see my motorcycle in a heap. My *new motorcycle!* I was so *mad,* I could feel the

Jesse and Cathy Duplantis

Tabasco sauce creeping up my legs. I'd just opened my mouth to say something, when I saw Kenneth and Gloria looking down at us. I changed my confession really fast.

"Glory to God!" I said, weakly.

I was so *embarrassed*.

"Are y'all OK?" Kenneth called.

I was still spitting dirt out of my mouth when Gloria grinned and said, "Would you do that *again*, Jesse? I didn't have my video on."

I just sputtered.

Kenneth tried to be nice. "Look," he said, "all of us have dropped a motorcycle at least once."

Yeah, they've all done it.

"Of course," he added, shaking with laughter, "we *all* saw *you* do it!"

Yeah, and they haven't *ever* let me forget it, either.

Being friends with Kenneth and Gloria is very *beneficial* to me. But it isn't always easy, because I'm Cajun.

Cajuns have hot tempers. I've been known to have an occasional fit of carnality.

It seems like every time we've got those motorcycle trailers packed down and locked, the women God gave us remember something *else* they need out of the thing.

Lock it.

Unlock it.

Lock it.

Unlock it.

We were somewhere up in Wyoming and I thought I was *finished*. I had locked the trailer and covered the whole bike—which takes a lot of time.

I'd no sooner finished than I realized I'd left my gloves in the trailer.

I was so *mad* at myself.

I was *boiling*.

I was so mad, I forgot that Kenneth and Gloria Copeland were standing on one side of me, and Dennis Burke was standing on the other.

"I'll tell you what," I stormed. "I'm constantly locking that thing without thinking." Suddenly I realized I was using my own words to perpetuate the problem. That irritated me even more. "I tell you, this negative confession is *killing me!*" I said.

Kenneth Copeland literally fell on the sidewalk. "Jesse!"

Oh yeah, I ought not to say my confession is killing me in front of Kenneth and Gloria. I forgot.

That's what I mean when I say it's beneficial, but not always easy.

They laid into me like crazy.

If you're laughing at me right now, watch out. Fits of carnality aren't limited to Cajuns.

Have *you* had one today?

Jesse Duplantis

I've noticed over the years that Kenneth and I like a lot of the same foods. When we stop at a Chinese restaurant, for example, we usually order the same thing off the menu. With one exception.

I love hot food. I love peppers, Tabasco and anything spicy. So I tell the waitress, "I want mine smoking hot!"

Kenneth orders the same thing, but tells her, "I don't want *any* peppers on it."

One time the waitress mixed up our orders.

The two plates *looked* the same.

Kenneth took a bite and it burned all the hairs off his nose.

It was fun to see what he would have looked like as a Cajun. He had Tabasco coming up his legs and smoke coming out his ears.

After seeing that, I decided that Kenneth *is* Cajun.

When he's preaching under the anointing of God…he's *smoking!*

J e s s e   D u p l a n t i s

I've always wanted to look like a *bad* biker. It seems that no matter how scruffy I look, though, people recognize me. I'll tell you something that may surprise you—that's not the case with Kenneth Copeland.

Sometimes we've been on the road so long we get dirt ground into our teeth. Our clothes get so dirty we've been known to mail them home. In addition to that, when Kenneth ties this rag around his head, he looks *bad*.

We'd been traveling quite a while one day, and it was getting hot. Kenneth called me on the CB.

"Hey, listen," he said, "take this exit. There's a little stand where we can get something to drink."

"10-4!"

We got in there and a guy walked up to me and said, "You're Jesse Duplantis!"

"Yeah…." I admitted. He started blessing God and talking about

Kenneth Copeland. Kenneth was standing *beside* me, listening. Finally, I pointed my finger at Gloria.

The man looked past Kenneth and said, *"You're* Gloria Copeland!"

Kenneth just stood there.

He looked like a member of Hell's Angels.

Finally, I had to do it. I pointed at Kenneth.

"That's Kenneth Copeland," I said.

The man almost fell on the ground.

It's funny when you think about it. Only the Holy Ghost could make a man look so good when he's in church and so *bad* when he's on a bike. But I can tell you this, whether he's in a fancy suit or leathers, when he opens his mouth and starts talking about Jesus there's no question in anyone's mind—that's Kenneth Copeland.

Jesse Duplantis

Jesse, Cathy and Kenneth take a break during a motorcycle trip.

One of the loneliest highways in the world is the one that stretches through the Nevada desert. And it's *hot.* We got out in the middle of that desert one day, and a road crew shut down all the traffic.

Nothing was moving in any direction.

People were just sitting there steaming in the heat.

We didn't get upset about being out there in the desert on motorcycles.

We parked those puppies and opened the ice chest.

We got comfortable, ate crab meat and drank Perrier.

You see, we're *Word* people.

We didn't have to wait to get *through* the desert to get to the promised land. We *live* in the promised land.

And so should *you.*

Jesse Duplantis

Photo Album

Kenneth and Gloria with
Shirley and Pat Boone

Rev. and Mrs. Kenneth Hagin Sr.,
Kenneth and Gloria, and Rev.
and Mrs. Kenneth Hagin Jr.

Charles Capps and Kenneth
share the Word.

In 1997, Jerry, Kenneth and Jesse ministered in the
Marshall Islands.

Kenneth and Gloria with Johnny Cash

Jesse and Cathy Duplantis, Kenneth and Gloria, and
Vikki and Dennis Burke

Kenneth with Willie George and cast members from *The Gunslinger*

Kenneth and Gloria with Creflo and Taffi Dollar

Kenneth and Mylon Le Fevre on the set of *Armor of Light*.

(clockwise): Gloria and Kenneth, Dennis and Vikki Burke, Cathy and Jesse Duplantis, Jerry and Carolyn Savelle

Memorable Moments

This is My name forever, and this is My memorial to all generations. EXODUS 3:15

I decided years ago, that if the Lord ever let me minister to children, I'd supply them with plenty of adventure. When my mother took me to church as a child, I was so bored that I just dreamed of adventure. That's why we do adventure videos like *Covenant Rider* and *Commander Kellie and the Superkids*SM.

Think about it, Hollywood is spending hundreds of millions of dollars to reach your 4- and 5-year-olds. And the church is trying to compete with that by giving them a 29-cent quarterly.

Do you think that's going to work?

I don't think so.

I remember a few years ago when Kellie introduced the first audiotape of *Commander Kellie and the Superkids*SM. Later in that service, Kellie was at the book table still dressed in her Commander Kellie uniform.

A little guy walked up to the table. He could barely see over it. "Commander Kellie!" he said, "I want adventure *so bad!*" He was almost beside himself.

Our Sunday schools need to be an adventure for our kids. And if you get into God, He'll build an adventure of faith for the boys and girls that will absolutely set their spirits and their minds on fire.

(Facing page) Kenneth portrays Wichita Slim in a scene from the children's adventure movie, *The Treasure of Eagle Mountain.*

When that happens, you don't have to beg them to learn.

Actually, the same thing is true for adults. Every human heart—young or old—has a hunger for adventure. Most of the time, a mundane life of unbelief and fear rips the adventure out of a person's heart and soul. It squelches it until their life is boiled down to a few hours a day doing something they don't want to do.

That's not the way God created man.

The book of Ephesians says that He ordains our paths, that He has developed paths that we should walk in, and have adventure.

God is the greatest adventurer of all time. If your life hasn't become a daily adventure, you haven't stepped over into *faith*.

K e n n e t h

Commander Kellie, the Superkids and Techno

Jesse Duplantis as the evil Saul Gillespie in *Covenant Rider.*

Brother Copeland phoned me one day and said, "Jesse, would you like to be in a movie?"

"I've never been in a movie," I said. "I don't know anything about acting."

"Why don't you read the script and see what you think about the part?" he asked.

I agreed to do it.

When they sent me the script, I sat down right away to read it. Then I called Kenneth. "This is the *worst* guy in the whole movie! This is an *evil* person! Why do you want me to play that part?"

"That's simple," Kenneth said with a chuckle, "we know your past."

We got a good laugh out of that, because my past doesn't bother me anymore than your past should bother you.

You may be thinking, "Yeah, Brother Jesse, but the *devil* knows my past and he talks to me about it."

That's OK. You can get rid of the devil. When he starts reminding you of your past, you just remind him of his *future!*

He'll get on his horse and ride as far from you as he can get...just like in the movies!

J e s s e   D u p l a n t i s

*A*nd after the time is spent, saith the Lord, there is coming for you a great outpouring of the supernatural—not to just bless the Church, but to cause a great awakening throughout the earth and in all lands, in all tongues, and in all peoples, in order to gather the precious fruit of the earth. For the time is at hand for all things to be fulfilled.

The time is at hand for the Word of the Lord to come to pass. The time is at hand for fulfillment. The time is at hand for those things that God has promised you as individuals to be fulfilled and be manifest. The time is at hand. The time is come and now is, saith the Lord, for great, great, great manifestations far beyond anything that has happened in the past. Not just beyond, but far beyond anything that's happened before now.

"Well, Brother Copeland, I've heard that before." Well, you're hearing it again. And it's

time, the Lord is saying. It is time. And it's time for congregations to take the responsibility to close in, in faith. Close in. Do you know what I mean by closing in? Do you know what they say when the police come? The FBI is closing in on them, Brother. It's time for God's forces to close in on the devil. Close in and tighten up its ranks, and begin to praise and worship God like never before, to begin to praise and shout the praises unto God.

For the strongholds of the devil are not strongholds with a base and foundation of power. For he has no power. His house is divided and he has already fallen. It's

The Berlin Wall fell on November 10, 1989.

just a matter of time until his strongholds come down like the walls of Jericho. But not without the shout of God's people, not without the obedience of God's people, and not without the strength and faith of those that call Him Lord.

These are the days of mighty, mighty importance, saith God. There are times in the ages to come when you will recall these days and these hours. And you'll read about them. And you'll see all that's going on from My perspective, saith the Lord. And you'll shake your head and say, "My, my, why didn't I do more? Why didn't I do more than what I was doing then? Couldn't I tell the mighty move of God, and the mighty hand of the Spirit was waving across the land like never before? Why didn't I pray more? Why didn't I move in closer into the inner circle of God's movings and God's things, and even the secrets of God would have been manifest in my heart. And I would have walked and talked and stood before God in a much more vibrant way."

Well, the time has come. We don't have to wait and wish that later, thank God. We can move into it now. We can move into it now.

Now this is what the Lord is saying, so hearken and heed it. Take heed to it. Listen. For a mighty wave of the supernatural is coming, and soon to burst on the scene, soon to crash like a mighty tidal wave, and burst on the scene...not just here and there, and a little here and a little there, but as a mighty

wave splashes and covers entire continents. And the power of God will rise in places that people didn't even know that there was a God. But it will be there. And there will be things that will fall before the pressure of it. That people will shake their head and say, "I never would have believed that could happen."

There are going to be political walls, and political fences that crumble right before men's eyes. Mighty, mighty strongholds of political power and political strength in different political systems all over the world will suddenly change hands, crumble and fall. And men will say, "I never would have thought that would happen, but I'm seeing it. I'm looking at it."

The Berlin Wall will come down.

It's a sign.

The Berlin Wall will come down.

There will be other walls that will come down. There will be some walls that will go up. Many changes are going to take place. But those that are wise in their hearts, and listen to the Spirit of God, will be quick to say, "Oh, the Lord is at work in the land."

And they will be quick to pray. And they will be quick to rise up as a witness in the streets. And they will be quick to testify wherever they go: "The Lord is working! The Lord is working! He'll save you! He'll lead you! He'll heal you! He'll deliver you! He'll bring you into the place that you ought to be."

I'll never forget the day, years ago, when a little runt of a fellow came to my office and wanted to see me. I knew his folks, so I let him in.

He was excited!

"Oh, Brother Copeland," he said, "I've been listening to your tapes, and I've quit my job!"

I just grinned. "Is that right?"

"Yes, amen! I'm living by faith! I'm out on faith! I'm going into the ministry full time!"

I didn't say it out loud, but I thought, *Lord, this guy can't preach his way out of a paper sack! He's gonna be back through here before long begging for money!*

The Lord spoke to me instantaneously, *Well, when he does, give him some.*

"Excuse me?"

When he does, give him some.

The Lord taught me something that day. He taught me never to sit in judgment of another man's faith.

Sure there will be times when you think someone isn't going to succeed in some faith project. When that happens, what you'd better do is pray, get in there and believe God. If you don't think they have the faith to carry this off, get in there and add your faith to it.

But *never* kick the feet out from under another person's faith.

I didn't know what I was talking about when I thought that young man wouldn't make it. But by acting in honor instead of dishonor, I opened the door for his success and *mine*.

The minute he walked out the door, the Lord said, *I'm commanding you and commissioning you to help teach and train this young man. You see to him, and see that he makes it.*

What would you and I have missed if I had tried to talk that boy out of the call on his life?

I would have talked him back into that automobile body shop he owned. But the Lord stopped me.

I sure am glad He did. That young man was *Jerry Savelle*.

K e n n e t h

I was in the West Indies years ago, off up in the mountains of Jamaica, in a place where nobody had seen a light-skinned man. The oldest man in the whole region was the pastor of a little church in the valley. The mountains rose steeply on either side of the church. There were steep, steep steps leading from the church, up the side of the mountain, to his home. He lived in a hand-hewn rock house with his daughter, son-in-law and his granddaughter.

When I got there, this old gentleman was sick, and everybody thought it was unto death. He was as close to dead as you could get and still be breathing. I could tell as soon as I arrived that he'd just quit. He was sick, and tired, and ready to turn his work over to the young folks.

The people in that church had been fasting and praying one day a week for a year that God would send them someone to bring them revelation knowledge of the New Testament. I wound up there at the end of their year-long time of fasting and prayer.

I climbed up to his house, sat down by his bed and talked to him for a while. I laid hands on him and prayed. I didn't say anything profound or deeply theological. I just started talking to the man about Jesus. I started telling him about my victories. I told him about victory, after victory, after victory.

A couple of days went by and he didn't come to the meetings. He couldn't get out of bed. I'd come to his room, pat him on the shoulder and say, "Oh, glory be to Jesus, there's no telling what we're liable to see here. There's no telling what God's likely to do before we get through." I'd just sit there and talk to him like that for a while, then I said, "I know you've seen many things in your day."

"Yes," he said, "I have."

"Tell me about it," I urged.

"Well, I tell you, Brother Copeland," he said with his strong Jamaican accent, then he started telling me about his victories in the Lord.

"Glory to God!" I said, "there's no telling what's liable to happen before we're through here."

The next evening, he was at church. "You're going to die!" the people told him.

"Well," he said, "I'm going to die down here rather than up there."

He'd put dying aside. He didn't want to miss what God was doing.

It was a good thing, because God showed up at those meetings.

I noticed that the people didn't seem too excited that God was moving among them. I discovered that for hundreds of years those mountain folk had been taught never to show emotion. They didn't want to offend me by getting excited and showing emotion.

One lady came up to me after a service and said, "Brother Copeland?"

"Yes."

"I want to praise the Lord, please."

"OK," I said, "what's the Lord done for you?"

"When I came tonight, I was blind. Now I see. Thank you."

Then she turned and walked off.

I turned to one of the elders there and asked, "Does she mean she was blind to the *Word*, and now she sees?"

"Oh, no, Brother Copeland," he said, "she could see nothing with her eyes."

That's all she said, "I was blind, and now I see. Thank you."

By the end of the week the pastor was in every meeting, and he was still telling his stories of victory.

When I arrived, I thought his granddaughter was about 12 years old. In fact, she was 18. She hadn't grown right because of a rheumatic heart, and she still looked like a little girl. It really got to me, because every few minutes her parents let her know she was dying. It wasn't my household, so I didn't say anything about it. I wasn't there to tell them how to treat their daughter.

That girl would reach over to pick something up, and someone would say, "Oh, darling, don't pick that up. Don't, Baby, now you know you're liable to fall dead any minute. You know what they said about your heart. Your heart isn't any good. Now, you just sit down here."

They wouldn't let her do anything!

They didn't know any better than to do that. They just called things that were as they were. It was toward the middle of the week when we went down the mountain for a service. They didn't let the girl go because the climb was too strenuous. When the meeting was over, people started climbing that path back up to the pastor's house to visit. I was still at the church when I heard the most blood-curdling scream. It was a terrible sound.

"My baby's dead! My baby's dead!"

What happened next is as vivid in my mind today as it was the moment it happened.

When she screamed, I was standing one step away from that rock stairway leading up to the house. I turned and started up there. I remember putting my foot on the first rock step, and when I lifted my foot for the next step, it came down squarely on their front porch.

God instantly picked me up and put me on the porch.

It seemed the most normal thing in the world.

A lot of people were already there, and I've never heard as much screaming and hollering in my life. Everyone was screaming. The girl's mother was running around in a circle screaming, *"My baby's dead!"*

The girl's father had picked her up. He held her so that her head was on his chest. His eyes were glazed over, and he was clearly in shock. My faith was on because I'd been preaching and ministering. Besides that, I just never let my faith have a vacation. But when I stepped into that commotion, I was under the

God moved mightily in the services in Jamaica.

influence of more than my own faith. The *gift* of faith had been added to my own.

There was a man with me who was a retired marine officer. I turned around to him and said, "Earl, shut that bunch up, and get them out on the front porch!"

"You got it, Boss!"

His military training took over. He shut those people up in a heartbeat. Then he herded them outside. Within 30 seconds my problems with those people were over. He got them outside and said, "Now, gather hands around. We shall pray in tongues."

Every one of them started praying in tongues.

I reached over and caught the girl's hand. It was cold and didn't want to move. I realized she must have died quite a while before, because her body was already set. I went ahead and checked for a pulse.

There was *nothing*.

She was stone cold, dead and stiff.

I stood there looking at her, and on the inside I thought, *Lord what do You want me to do?*

He didn't answer. He just acted.

Before my mind could get in gear to oppose Him, Jesus reared up inside of me. The words that welled up in me seemed bigger than I am, and seemed to come from someplace other than inside me. "In the Name of Jesus, I speak *life* to you. Now *walk!*"

Nothing.

All of a sudden, from somewhere down deep inside me, I got mad. I got mad at death. I got mad at hell. I got mad at the devil. "I said, *walk!*"

Nothing.

The boldness of the Lion of the tribe of Judah began to roll on the inside of me. The Bible says that Jesus was moved with compassion. That same compassion welled up in me and moved me.

I still held her by the hand, but now I let go and stepped back.

"I SAID IN THE NAME OF JESUS…*WALK!*"

She coughed, opened her eyes, and said, "Papa?"

She rose up out of her daddy's arms, alive, healed and filled with the Holy Ghost!

That group outside ran for their lives. "Oooh, she's a haint! There's a haint among us!"

They thought she was a ghost.

After her granddaddy got through

Kenneth with
Berrin Dixon, the
girl who was raised
from the dead.

with them, those people knew how to treat a miracle of God. He was around 75 years old at the time. By the way, before those meetings were over, he'd given up the idea of dying. He decided to stay around a while. When he was 78,

he put speakers on his car and drove all over those mountains preaching the gospel.

That girl, Berrin Dixon was her name, went down to Spanish Town in Jamaica and finished her education. Then, she went back into the mountains. The last time I heard from her she was teaching school, and Bible, to a bunch of little kids in the mountains.

When I think back on those days in Jamaica, I think of something Smith Wigglesworth said. "Give me five more minutes of that anointing. I'd rather have it than a gold fence built around the whole world 10 feet high."

A lot of you are going to experience that kind of anointing and that kind of glory in the days ahead, because it's on us right now. There is a higher degree of it all the time now than there was back then. I'm experiencing more of it now in meetings that I preach than I have in all my life and ministry.

I like the question Paul asked in Acts 26:8, *"Why should it be thought a thing incredible with you, that God should raise the dead?"*

I'll take it a step further.

Don't think it an incredible thing that God should raise the dead…*through you!*

Kenneth

Now unto Him that is able to do exceeding abundantly beyond all we ask or think, according to the power that works in us.

To Him be glory in the church and in Christ Jesus to all generations forever and ever.

Amen

From the Executive Director

We are told many times in the Bible to stop and remember what the Lord has done for us. We are told that, like Joshua, we should build memorials to God for future generations.

But having done that, we must not camp there.

We must go on to do what God has commissioned us to do. We must go in His might and in His power to take the promised land.

With the help of our Partners, that is what all of us here at Kenneth Copeland Ministries are determined to do. We are determined to press on toward the mark of our high calling in Christ Jesus and fulfill the mission God has given us.

What is that mission? It is this:

We are called to lead people, primarily born-again believers, to the place where they operate proficiently in the biblical principles of faith, love, healing, prosperity, redemption and righteousness, and to the place

where they can share those principles with others.

We are called to assist believers in becoming rooted, grounded and established in the Word of God by teaching them to give God's Word first place in their lives (Colossians 1:23; Psalm 112).

We are called to reveal the mysteries, the victorious revelations of God's Word, that have been hidden from the ages (Colossians 1:25-28).

We are called to build a spiritual army of mature believers, bringing them from milk to meat, from religion to reality. We are called to train them to become skillful in the Word of righteousness, to stand firm in spiritual warfare against the kingdom of darkness (Hebrews 5:12-14; Ephesians 6:10-18).

We are called to proclaim that "Jesus is Lord" from the top of the world to the bottom and all the way around.

So onward we go, in the Spirit and power of God, arm in arm with the Partners He has given us, thanking God for His faithfulness as we continue along our journey of faith!

John Copeland
Executive Director
Kenneth Copeland Ministries

Prayer for Salvation and Baptism in the Holy Spirit

Heavenly Father, I come to You in the Name of Jesus. Your Word says, *"Whosoever shall call on the name of the Lord shall be saved"* (Acts 2:21). I am calling on You. I pray and ask Jesus to come into my heart and be Lord over my life according to Romans 10:9-10. *"If thou shalt confess with thy mouth the Lord Jesus, and shalt believe in thine heart that God hath raised him from the dead, thou shalt be saved."* I do that now. I confess that Jesus is Lord, and I believe in my heart that God raised Him from the dead.

I am now reborn! I am a Christian—a child of Almighty God! I am saved! You also said in Your Word, *"If ye then, being evil, know how to give good gifts unto your children: HOW MUCH MORE shall your heavenly Father give the Holy Spirit to them that ask him?"* (Luke 11:13). I'm also asking You to fill me with the Holy Spirit. Holy Spirit, rise up within me as I praise God.

I fully expect to speak with other tongues as You give me the utterance (Acts 2:4).

Begin to praise God for filling you with the Holy Spirit. Speak those words and syllables you receive—not in your own language, but the language given to you by the Holy Spirit. You have to use your own voice. God will not force you to speak. Worship and praise Him in your heavenly language—in other tongues.

Continue with the blessing God has given you and pray in tongues each day.

You are a born-again, Spirit-filled believer. You'll never be the same!

Find a good Word of God preaching church, and become a part of a church family who will love and care for you as you love and care for them.

We need to be hooked up to each other. It increases our strength in God. It's God's plan for us.

Kenneth and Gloria
Copeland, 1996
Eagle Mountain
Motorcycle Rally.

About Kenneth and Gloria Copeland

Kenneth and Gloria Copeland are the best-selling authors of more than 60 books such as *Managing God's Mutual Funds* and *Living Contact*, published in 1997. Together they have co-authored other books including *Family Promises* and the popular devotional *From Faith to Faith—A Daily Guide to Victory.* As founders of Kenneth Copeland Ministries in Fort Worth, Texas, Kenneth and Gloria are in their 30th year of circling the globe with the uncompromised Word of God, preaching and teaching a lifestyle of victory for every Christian.

Their daily and weekly *Believer's Voice of Victory* television broadcasts now air on nearly 500 stations around the world, and their *Believer's Voice of Victory* and *Shout!* magazines are sent to nearly 700,000 adults and children worldwide. Their international prison ministry reaches an average of 60,000 new inmates every year and receives more than 30,000 pieces of correspondence each month. With offices and staff in the United States, Canada, England, Australia, South Africa and Ukraine, Kenneth and Gloria's teaching materials—books, magazines, audio and videotapes—have been translated into at least 22 languages to reach the world with the love of God.

World Offices
of Kenneth Copeland Ministries

For more information about KCM and a free catalog,
please write the office nearest you:

Kenneth Copeland Ministries, Fort Worth, Texas 76192-0001

Kenneth Copeland
Locked Bag 2600
Mansfield Delivery Centre
QUEENSLAND 4122
AUSTRALIA

Kenneth Copeland
Post Office Box 15
BATH
BA1 1GD
ENGLAND

Kenneth Copeland
Private Bag X 909
FOUNTAINEBLEAU
2032
REPUBLIC OF SOUTH AFRICA

Kenneth Copeland
Post Office Box 378
Surrey
BRITISH COLUMBIA
V3T 5B6
CANADA

220123 MINSK
REPUBLIC OF BELARUS
Post Office 123
P/B 35
Kenneth Copeland Ministries